Lytton Strachey

Twayne's English Authors Series

Kinley E. Roby, Editor

Northeastern University

TEAS 462

LYTTON STRACHEY
(1880–1932)
Photograph courtesy The Strachey Trust

Lytton Strachey

By John Ferns

McMaster University

Twayne Publishers
A Division of G. K. Hall & Co. • *Boston*

Lytton Strachey
John Ferns

Copyright 1988 by G. K. Hall & Co.
All rights reserved.
Published by Twayne Publishers
A Division of G.K. Hall & Co.
70 Lincoln Street
Boston, Massachusetts, 02111

Copyediting supervised by Barbara Sutton
Book production by Janet Zietowski
Book design by Barbara Anderson

Typeset in 11 pt. Garamond
by Huron Valley Graphics, Inc., Ann Arbor, Michigan

Printed on permanent/durable acid-free paper
and bound in the United States of America

Library of Congress Cataloging in Publication Data

Ferns, John, 1941–
    Lytton Strachey / by John Ferns.
        p.   cm. — (Twayne's English authors series ; TEAS 462)
    Bibliography; p.
    Includes index.
    ISBN 0-8057-6966-8 (alk. paper)
    1. Strachey, Lytton, 1880–1932—Criticism and interpretation.
2. Biography (as a literary form) 3. Great Britain—History—20th
century. I. Title. II. Series.
PR6037.T73Z65 1988   87-28817
828'.91209–dc19   CIP

To Gill, Tom, Betsy and Carolyn

Contents

About the Author

John Ferns was born in 1941 in Ottawa, Ontario. He was educated at King Edward VI's School, Birmingham, and St. Edmund Hall, Oxford, where he received an Honours B.A. He received a Diploma in Education from the University of Nottingham and an M.A. and Ph.D. from the University of Western Ontario where he held a Commonwealth Scholarship, a Canada Council Pre-Doctoral Fellowship and a Queen Elizabeth II Scholarship.

Since 1970, Professor Ferns has been a member of the Faculty of Humanities at McMaster University, Hamilton, Ontario, where he now holds the position of Professor of English. During 1976–77 he held a Leave Fellowship from the Canada Council while on sabbatical leave at the Centre of Canadian Studies, University of Edinburgh, Scotland. In 1985–86 he was a Visiting Research Fellow in the Department of English and Comparative Literary Studies at the University of Warwick, England, while holding a Leave Fellowship from the Social Sciences and Humanities Research Council of Canada. From 1982 to 1985 he was Associate Dean of Humanities (Studies) at McMaster. He has published an earlier study in Twayne's World Authors Series on Canadian poet, critic, and anthologist, A. J. M. Smith. He is the author of four volumes of poetry: *The Antlered Boy* (1970), *Henry Hudson* (1975), *The Snow Horses* (1977), and *From The River* (1985). With Brian Crick he is coeditor of George Whalley's *Studies in Literature and the Humanities: Innocence of Intent* (1985).

Preface

Lytton Strachey, the early twentieth-century critic and biographer, is best known for *Eminent Victorians* (1918), in which he attempts to "debunk" such important Victorians as Cardinal Manning, Florence Nightingale, Dr. Arnold, and General Gordon. The present study does not depart from the commonly held view that this is Strachey's liveliest, though surely not his most responsible, work. The study discusses the development of Strachey's entire career as a writer, both what preceded and what followed *Eminent Victorians* (1918).

Strachey's major achievement as a writer was his contribution to what came to be known as the "new biography." This involved a rejection of the standard Victorian two-volume biographies that consisted of a life and letters, in favor of the development of shorter, more psychologically oriented, and sharply written lives. All three of Strachey's major biographical works—*Eminent Victorians* (1918), *Queen Victoria* (1921), and *Elizabeth and Essex* (1928)—follow this new form of biography. *Elizabeth and Essex,* in particular, owes a debt to the psychology of Sigmund Freud. Lytton Strachey is chiefly remembered as an iconoclast who sought to exchange conservative Victorian for more liberal, modern values. Satire and wit were his principle weapons in this enterprise.

Scholarship on Strachey accumulated slowly in the decades following his death. His younger brother, James, aided and encouraged scholarly inquiry into his brother's life and work. In 1948, he edited a six-volume *Collected Works* published by Chatto and Windus and in 1956, with Leonard Woolf, the letters of Virginia Woolf and Lytton Strachey. The last four decades have seen the publication of four important works on Lytton Strachey: the American scholar C. R. Sanders's *Lytton Strachey: His Mind and Art* (1957); the English biographer Michael Holroyd's definitive *Lytton Strachey: A Critical Biography* (1967–68); the French scholar Gabriel Merle's *Lytton Strachey (1880–1932): biographe et critique d'un critique et biographe* (1980), and Michael Edmonds's *Lytton Strachey: A Bibliography* (1981).

The present volume contributes to Strachey scholarship by providing, in a single volume, a critical study of Strachey's development as a writer in relation to his life. The approach taken will be to show how Strachey's more important biographical work grew out of his earlier creative and critical work. I have been allowed, through the generosity of the Strachey Trust, to quote from Strachey's unpublished letters to illuminate this development. The study will show how Strachey's increasing dissatisfaction with the need for judgment in literary criticism, his lack of success as novelist, poet, or playwright together with his obsession with people led him to become a psychologically oriented biographer. His critical rejection of the Victorians in *Eminent Victorians* (1918), as will be shown, also grew out of his opposition to World War I for which he held his father's Victorian generation responsible.

John Ferns

McMaster University

Acknowledgments

For various forms of assistance in the preparation of this book I owe thanks to many people: Dr. Laurel Braswell, Dr. Andrew Brink and Dr. Howard Jones of McMaster University, Dr. Anne Bolgan and Dr. John Graham of the University of Western Ontario, and Dr. S. P. Rosenbaum of the University of Toronto. Dr. Michael Bell of the Department of English and Comparative Literary Studies, University of Warwick, arranged a Visiting Research Fellowship for me at his university for the academic year 1985–86. McMaster University granted me the research leave, and the Social Sciences and Humanities Research Council of Canada provided me with a Leave Fellowship that enabled me to carry out the research. My wife Gill and children Tom, Betsy, and Carolyn gave me great support while the work was in progress.

Special thanks go to Professor Gabriel Merle of the Sorbonne, whose two-volume study, *Lytton Strachey (1880–1932): biographe et critique d'un critique et biographe* (Paris, 1980), has helped me every step of the way.

Finally, I wish to thank Mr. Michael Holroyd, coexecutor of The Strachey Trust for help received from his definitive biography of Lytton Strachey, for promptly and helpfully replying to my many questions, and for permission to quote from published and unpublished material.

Chronology

1880	Giles Lytton Strachey born Stowey House, Clapham Common, London, 1 March.
1884	Family moves to 69 Lancaster Gate, the family home until August 1907.
1889–1893	Attends Henry Forde's school at Parkstone, Poole, Dorset.
1892–1893	Travels with his sister Dorothy to Gibraltar, Cairo, and the Cape of Good Hope from 23 December 1892 to May 1893.
1893–1894	Attends Abbotsholme School.
1894–1896	Attends Leamington College.
1897–1899	Attends Liverpool University College.
1899	Admitted to Trinity College, Cambridge.
1902	Elected the 239th Apostle to the Cambridge Conversazione Society, 1 February. Receives the Chancellor's Medal for his poem "Ely: An Ode."
1903	Obtains second-class honors in part 2 of the History tripos.
1904	Submits dissertation on Warren Hastings in hope of gaining fellowship at Trinity College, Cambridge, 1 September. Not successful.
1905	Fails to win Le Bas Prize for long essay on English Letter Writers, May. Relationship with Duncan Grant begins, summer. Again submits dissertation, 1 September; again refused.
1907	Joins staff of the *Spectator* at the suggestion of the editor, his cousin, St. Loe Strachey, June.
1908	Father, Sir Richard Strachey, dies 12 February. Works on articles for the *Spectator* and the *New Quarterly*, discovers the relationship between Duncan Grant and J. M. Keynes, July.

1909	Proposes marriage to Virginia Stephen and then withdraws the proposal, 17 February. Elected to the Savile Club, 31 March. Seeks health cure in Sweden, July–September.
1911	Begins relationship with Henry Lamb.
1912	*Landmarks in French Literature* published. Writes play "A Son of Heaven." Begins to write article on Madame du Deffand and conceives idea of *Victorian Silhouettes* (later *Eminent Victorians*), October.
1913	Portrait painted by Henry Lamb. Writes *Ermyntrude and Esmeralda,* February–March.
1914	Works on Cardinal Manning portrait for *Eminent Victorians.*
1915	Works on Florence Nightingale portrait, January–June. Meets Dora Carrington, begins Dr. Arnold portrait, November.
1916	Demands exemption from military service and reads declaration of conscientious objection. Exemption rejected, 7 March. Exempted from military service following medical examination, 10 April. Begins General Gordon portrait, October.
1917	Established at The Mill House, Tidmarsh, with Carrington. Chatto and Windus accept *Eminent Victorians,* December.
1918	*Eminent Victorians* published. Ralph Partridge arrives at Tidmarsh, 10 August.
1920	Works on *Queen Victoria.*
1921	*Queen Victoria* published. Ralph Partridge and Carrington marry 21 May.
1922	*Books and Characters* published. Attends conference in Berlin with brother James at which Freud speaks, September.
1923	Ralph Partridge meets Frances Marshall and eventually separates from Carrington.
1924	Moves into Ham Spray House, Hungerford, Berkshire, 7 August.

1925	Delivers Leslie Stephen Lecture at Cambridge on Pope, June. Two performances of "A Son of Heaven," 12–13 July. Begins work on *Elizabeth and Essex,* December.
1926	Receives honorary doctorate from University of Edinburgh, 18 July. Relationship with Roger Senhouse begins, August.
1927	Invited to edit the Greville Memoirs, 13 November.
1928	*Elizabeth and Essex* published. Mother, Jane Maria Strachey, dies, 15 December.
1930	Ill through January. Works on Greville Memoirs, May.
1931	*Portraits in Miniature* published. Carrington receives a prize from the *Week-end Review* for an obituary of Strachey. Strachey begins to write article on *Othello,* August. Makes a last visit to France of which he keeps a journal. Visits Brighton with Roger Senhouse, October. Becomes ill at London dinner party. Dr. Elinor Rendel diagnoses typhoid, November. Sir Maurice Cassidy diagnoses colitis and ulcer, 9 December. Professor Leonard Dudgeon and Dr. John Ryle called in.
1932	Sir Arthur Hurst called in. Strachey says that he has always wished to marry Carrington, 20 January. Carrington attempts suicide during the night of 20–21 January. Lytton Strachey dies 1:30 P.M., 21 January. Carrington commits suicide, 11 March.
1933	*Characters and Commentaries* published.

Chapter One

Life

Giles Lytton Strachey, the early twentieth-century biographer and critic, was born on 1 March 1880 at Stowey House, Clapham Common, London. He was the fourth son of Lieutenant-General Sir Richard and Lady Jane Maria Strachey, ten of whose thirteen children survived childhood. The Strachey family traced its ancestry back to the Elizabethan period and an original Sir Giles who, in Shakespeare's day, was involved in the war of the theaters and sailed to the Bermudas, about which he provided an account of his travels that Shakespeare drew upon in *The Tempest*.[1] In the eighteenth century the family became prominent in India where Sir Richard, who was born at the family seat, Sutton Court, Somerset, on 24 July 1817, spent his career. After training in the East India Company's military school, he joined the corps of Bombay engineers in 1839. His career in India, during which he was elected Fellow of the Royal Society for his plant and geological observations, and became director of Public Works for India, lasted for thirty-two years.

On 13 March 1840 his wife-to-be Jane Maria Grant, daughter of Sir John Peter Grant of Rothiemurchus, Scotland, was born aboard ship en route for India. The couple met after Richard Strachey became secretary to Sir John Peter in the India Public Works department in 1855. They were married on 4 January 1859. Richard was then forty-one and Jane Maria eighteen. Some of Lytton's older brothers and sisters were born in England, some in India, but Lieutenant-General Strachey left India in 1871 and by 1874 the family was settled at Stowey House, Clapham Common, London. When Lytton was born in 1880, his father was sixty-two and his mother thirty-nine. Lytton was brought up almost entirely by his mother, a strong-willed Scotswoman who wrote children's books, enjoyed English and French literature and the friendship of Carlyle, George Eliot, and Robert Browning. His father was a somewhat remote figure who studied engineering maps in his study and read novels by the fire, though he had been a highly organized and determined administrator during his India days. Domestic administration and the upbringing of children, however, he left increasingly to his wife. In 1884 the family moved to 69 Lancaster Gate in central London, which was to be Lytton Strachey's home for the next twenty-three years.[2]

Two years later Lytton and his younger sister Marjorie, who had been baptized together in 1883, began to attend the Hyde Park Kindergarten and School at 24 Chilworth Street where Lytton continued for the next eighteen months. His younger brother James, the translator of Freud, who was to become his lifelong confidant and eventual literary executor, was born in 1887, the last of the thirteen Strachey children. Lytton's early years of mother-directed activity, in which he was frequently dressed as a girl, consisted of a regimen of reading, writing, the learning of French from a French governess,[3] play, mainly with his sisters, and annual summer holidays at his mother's family home in the north of Scotland. At the age of nine Lytton was sent to boarding school for the first time, to Henry Forde at Parkstone in Poole, Dorset. The seaside setting may have been chosen because of Lytton's delicate health. His health remained delicate, and on 23 December 1892 he was sent with his older sister Dorothy on a five-month cruise aboard the *Coromandel* stopping at Gibraltar and Cairo before reaching the Cape of Good Hope by way of the Suez Canal. Lytton kept a diary of this trip.[4]

September 1893 saw the beginning of Lytton's brief and disastrous stay at Abbotsholme school in Derbyshire, which under the direction of Dr. Cecil Reddie administered to the body as well as to the mind. Lytton was unable to manage the regimen of farm work that was a part of the school's discipline. So, removing him from Abbotsholme, Lady Strachey placed her second youngest son in Leamington College for two years. Lytton's time there was, to begin with, thoroughly miserable. He was bullied and known as "Scraggs" because of his lanky thinness. Nevertheless, he passed his Oxford and Cambridge Lower Certificate examination a year later and in fall 1895 was named head of his house. It was at Leamington that he first fell in love with older, athletic-looking boys, whose prowess Lytton with his short sight and lack of coordination, could not equal, yet who he idealized and would like to have resembled.

At the age of seventeen, in October 1897, Lytton was entered into Liverpool University College where there was a family connection with the Professor of English, Sir Walter Raleigh, and where he was to spend the next two academic years. Illness continued, however, and in February 1898 he was forced to spend a three-week convalescence in the country. The extent of Lytton's self-loathing is revealed in a diary that he began almost immediately after his eighteenth Birthday:

> My self-conscious vanity is really most painful. As I walk through the streets I am agonised by the thoughts of my appearance. Of course it is hideous, but what *does* it matter? I only make it worse by peering into people's faces to see what they are thinking. And the worst of it is that I hate myself for doing it. The truth is I want *companionship* . . . I wonder if I shall ever "fall in love." I can't help smiling at the question—if they only knew—if they only knew! But it is a tragedy also.(*SP*, 99–100)

This had been preceded by an entry about a week earlier on 3 March 1898 in which he writes "my character is not yet crystalized" and then proceeds to project his feelings of cynicism and disgust onto Shakespeare. Strachey, perhaps aware of the Keatsian idea of "negative capability," believed at this time that Shakespeare had no character. Shakespeare, he thought, was "a mere receptacle" for impressions, believed in no gospel, not even in right and wrong, and was a skeptic and cynic. This surprising estimation of Shakespeare that projects Strachey's cynicism more than it does Shakespeare's, looks back to an earlier piece of writing undertaken at Leamington College on 13 November 1896 under the mask of a Sir John Snooks of Cambridge and in which Strachey seeks to justify his homosexuality through an appeal to Plato and, significantly, Shakespeare: "—I read for the first time. . .the Symposium. . .That day of surprise, relief, and fear to know that what I feel now was felt 2000 years ago in glorious Greece. . . . (I may be sinning, but I am doing so in the company of Shakespeare and Greece.)" (*SP,82*).

These earlier passages help us to understand what Strachey meant in his Liverpool diary on 11 March 1898. For Strachey's ambivalence was, indeed, his tragedy. Although he increasingly identified himself as a homosexual, he did "fall in love" with Dora Carrington, who suffered herself from ambivalent feelings. On his deathbed in January 1932 Strachey expressed the wish that he had married her. Carrington's suicide in March 1932 followed hard upon Strachey's death. So the agonizing diary entries of an eighteen-year-old university student expressed an early life of domination, anxiety, and feelings of physical ugliness and worthlessness. The small boy whose mother wished him to be viceroy of India (like his Lytton namesake the poet "Owen Meredith") or poet laureate, wondered at eighteen whether he could be

painted him. He had been traduced by his original accusers, and the
false view of Hastings had been continued by James Mill and Macaulay.
Strachey's work was part of an enterprise begun by Sir James Stephen
and his own uncle, Sir John Strachey, to restore the reputation of
Hastings. Cambridge reading parties continued, and at Easter he attended one at Lynton in Devon. This was followed by a three-week
holiday at the home of his sister Dorothy, who was now married to the
French painter Simon Bussy, at Roquebrune in the south of France.
Dorothy, who was fourteen years older than Lytton, had caused family
consternation by her marriage and had accompanied Lytton on his trip
to South Africa in 1893. Lytton admired her independence. She became
the translator of André Gide's novels and was herself the author of a
novel called *Olivia* by Olivia. Simon Bussy was to challenge Lytton
about his own career a couple of years later.

Lytton wrote to his friend Duncan Grant on 25 February 1906 about
Simon Bussy's challenge:

I didn't know what to do, I couldn't speak French, and even in English, what
could I have said?—
. . . .
How could I explain—Oh! What I can hardly explain even to you—my
utter inability to take "art" and "literature" and the whole bag of tricks,
seriously: . . . I nearly burst out to him—"*Je suis obsédé! Obsédé par les
personages!*" Only I didn't, because it couldn't have done any good and the
French seemed more than doubtful. . . .I went away half in tears, and
wanting to tell it all to you.[8]

The successful French painter wondered why his brother-in-law would
not commence a great work. Lytton was twenty-six and obsessed by
people—in particular by his relationship with his cousin Duncan
Grant—and unable at that time to take art and literature seriously,
even though he had earlier written to his cousin hoping that they would
always be great artists and great friends. But behind the beginning of
Strachey's passionate affair with Duncan Grant lay two failed attempts
to win a Trinity fellowship.

Following his 1904 holiday with the Bussys, Strachey pursued the
research for his Warren Hastings thesis in the British Museum through
May and June and submitted it on 1 September. However, at the end of
September he learned that he was not elected to a fellowship. He went

to recuperate in Rothiemurchus during October, the same month in which his university friend, Leonard Woolf, departed for Ceylon. The rest of the term he spent hovering about Cambridge trying to secure the election of Arthur Hobhouse (with whom he was "in love") to the Apostles. At the beginning of 1905, however, he discovered that a liaison was in progress between Hobhouse and J. M. Keynes. Hobhouse was elected to the society in February but in March Strachey ceased writing to Keynes. In May he learned that his long essay on English Letter Writers, which his brother James was later to include in *Characters and Commentaries* (1933), had failed to win the Le Bas prize.

That summer Strachey put a further three months' work into his Hastings dissertation with the intent of resubmitting it in the hope of securing a fellowship in the fall. Much of this work was done at Kettering where the Strachey family had rented a house. It was here in July–August that Strachey fell "in love" with his cousin Duncan Grant, a relationship that was to reach its height by the end of that year but was to end in despair and misery when Strachey was again "betrayed" by his "friend" J. M. Keynes when Keynes and Grant went off together in the summer of 1908. However, for the time being, Strachey again submitted his thesis for the Trinity fellowship at the end of August and learned again of his failure by the end of September. This time, however, he had the consolation of his affair with Grant. "But I feel, my most beloved, that there is nothing that really matters, so long as we're each other's. Don't you agree? Let's both be great artists and great friends," he writes to Duncan Grant on 9 October 1905. The fellowship seemed unimportant to Strachey in comparison to his relationship with Grant.

With his dissertation refused, Lytton left his room, K6, in Trinity to his brother James and returned to Lancaster Gate where he began his career as a journalist. A letter of 31 October to Duncan Grant indicates the transition that Strachey was making at this time. In it he mentions an unsuccessful attempt to persuade the publisher, Mr. Methuen, to accept his Warren Hastings thesis as a book. Also, he speaks of seeing a production of Ibsen's *The Wild Duck,* which indicates the involvement with dramatic reviewing that he was beginning. From about this time until the publication of his first book, *Landmarks in French Literature* in 1912, Strachey wrote over a hundred articles and reviews for journals such as Desmond MacCarthy's *New Quarterly* but, in particular, for his cousin St. Loe Strachey's the *Spectator* for which he wrote weekly and became drama critic. Strachey had written essays at Cambridge as an undergraduate and for the various societies of which he was a member. But this period, from 1906 until the beginning of World War I was really the time of his apprenticeship as a writer. Privately he wrote hundreds of letters to friends such as Duncan Grant, J. M. Keynes, Leonard Woolf, and his brother James; publicly he wrote reviews of books primarily on English and French literature, history, and drama.

During the first week of 1906 Strachey and Duncan Grant spent a happy week together at the home of their aunt, Lady Colville, at Ledbury. Duncan Grant was to go to Paris in February to study painting and Strachey accompanied him there, going on to spend the winter months at Menton in the south of France. In April Duncan Grant wrote to announce that, like Keynes earlier, he was in love with Hobhouse. This reduced Strachey to illness. He left Menton, and his sister Philippa looked after him in Paris where he paid daily visits to Duncan Grant. In May he returned to London where he was ill for three weeks.

October found him ensconced at Lancaster Gate writing book reviews. The death of Thoby Stephen on 21 November was a shock to the entire group of Cambridge friends and seemed to mark the end of a youthful period of college excitements and friendships. Strachey was seeing Keynes during November and December but was no longer in full sympathy with his one-time friend. The Hobhouse episode, to be reproduced in the Grant-Keynes liaison, had put an end to that.

Strachey's world was reduced to ashes in January 1907 when Duncan Grant returned to Paris on the 19th without saying goodbye. Strachey told him on the 20th that he felt "utterly crushed" and "nearly gave way altogether" when he learned of Grant's departure. Grant seemed to be the only person with whom Strachey could communicate and Grant was rejecting him. Strachey's letter of 20 January was desperate: "But my dear, who am I to tell things to unless it's to you? I used to tell Keynes nearly everything, but his common sense was enough to freeze a volcano. . . . " Yet three days earlier, *before* Grant's unfriendly departure, Strachey had written, "Oh if I'd only been a woman! But alas! alas!" and then continued:

> "Wordsworth says—
> 'Beyond participation lie
> My troubles, and beyond relief;
> If any chance to heave a sigh
> They pity me and not my grief.' "[9]

Wordsworth's sorrows can be traced back to his early loss of his parents;
Strachey, both of whose parents were still alive in 1907, seems equally,
through Wordsworth, to express a sense of loss or lack of possession of
any firm sense of emotional attachment or security. There were in his
life his aged study-bound, novel-reading father and overtaxed mother
packing him off on cruises and to schools. Strachey, weakened by
anxiety and with his sexual identity confused by the already noted
"cross-dressing," turned from unsatisfactory parental relationships to
overidealized relationships with "friends" that (such was the pattern of
his emotional life) led only to further rejection and suffering. The
extremity of Strachey's dependence, for example, seems to have caused
Grant to reject him.

Ironically, Strachey's self-hatred and indifference to women made
him attractive to some women, and while he was staying at Kingsham
with the Homere sisters in January 1907, Angelica Homere showed
him some attention that he hysterically rejected. Nevertheless, in February he participated somewhat distantly in his sister Philippa's suffrag-
ette activities since he took the view that universal buggery would
assure women's liberation.

In June his cousin St. Loe invited him to join the staff of the
Spectator. This was the real beginning of Strachey's life as a writer, and
when the burden of his emotions became unbearable, he could often, in
these years, lose himself in work. In the late 1920s, however, as he
aged and weakened, this avenue of escape became less and less possible
to him. Externally, his was or should have been a pleasant enough life,
but Strachey was twenty-seven years old. His career as a writer was only
just beginning and he had not completed any great work. In truth, he
did not believe himself capable of such production. Strachey's transi-
tional situation in life was underscored at this time by his family's
removal from his childhood home, Lancaster Gate, to Belsize Park
Gardens, Hampstead. Duncan Grant returned from France in the fall,
and by Christmas their relationship was restored with walks together
on Hampstead Heath.

In January 1908 Strachey declined his cousin St. Loe's offer of the
editorship of the *Spectator.* That such an offer was made must surely
qualify our sense of the state of hopeless weakness that Strachey projects
in his letters to Duncan Grant. St. Loe was a practical man of affairs and
Lytton was able to tailor his writing to suit St. Loe's needs as James
Strachey has shown. [10] Clearly, Lytton was able to compromise with the
literary world. He would not have become the popularly successful

writer he became if he had not been able to effect such a compromise. His cousin clearly had a confidence in Strachey as a practical man that Strachey himself lacked.

On 12 February his father Sir Richard died at the age of ninety. Strachey did not go to the south of France this year, and although he joined Moore's reading party at Easter, he kept to his room in May working hard on his reviews for the *Spectator* and the *New Quarterly*. At twenty-eight some iron was beginning to enter Strachey's soul, and although he spent almost all of June at King's College, Cambridge, he was producing a review a week.

It was in July that he discovered the liaison between Grant and Keynes. Although his response to this betrayal was violent and produced his usual illness, his account of the experience to his brother James and his subsequent ironic response to the whole affair requires careful consideration. On 17 July 1908 after a meeting with Keynes he writes to his brother James as follows:

Unfortunately I was too honest, and had a fit, which at last did make him begin very dimly to realise that it was perhaps rather odd and important that he was "in love." I think ever since the Hobber days there's been distinct deterioration. Then, there was certainly just a touch of romance; and now the hardness is quite complete.

.   .   .   .

I really think, though, that as far as I'm concerned the worst of it is now over, and I shall regain comparative equanimity.[11]

The final, brief paragraph is crucial here since four days later Strachey, again writing to his brother, appears to have gained a sense of detachment aided, perhaps, by thoughts of the philosophy of G. E. Moore: "Friendship has a meaning—don't you believe that?—and, in this kind of muddle, all that one can do is to act as a friend and be—well, if not 'generous' at least decent. If you don't follow me, I shan't be surprised, but I hope you do." It is clear from his published writings how catty and even dishonest Strachey could be, yet in this last passage to his brother the self-sacrificing kindness and gentleness that was the other side of his deeply, and unhappily, divided nature can be seen. Although Strachey was betrayed by Grant and Keynes and other homosexual lovers throughout his life, he could also inspire loyalty and love in, for example, his brother James and Dora Carrington.

While Duncan Grant and Keynes set off for the Orkneys at the end of July, Strachey and James spent the month of August at Rothiemurchus from where they perpetrated an elaborate hoax on Grant and Keynes detailing an encounter with a homosexual lover named Horace Townsend who was subsequently reported to have drowned. It was Strachey's idea of comic-ironic revenge upon his erstwhile friends. September, however, found Strachey weakened by the whole episode and suffering from intestinal trouble.

On 7 January 1909 he attended a literary dinner with Virginia Stephen and her cousin, the historian H. A. L. Fisher. This was to have a happy issue for Strachey about eighteen months later when Fisher invited him to write a "panoramic" study of French literature for the Home University Library series, which became Strachey's first book. Clearly the relationship with Virginia Stephen was important to Strachey at this time for, perhaps on the rebound from Grant and Keynes, he made a reckless attempt to balance his life by asking her, on 17 February, to marry him. Although Virginia accepted him, Strachey, perhaps realizing the impossibility of what he was offering, withdrew his offer almost as soon as it was made.

In March Keynes was elected a Fellow of King's College, and Strachey was elected to the Savile Club. The remainder of the year was a mixture of reviewing and rather ineffectual gadding about. In April he decided that he ought to leave home. However, he became ill and had to spend a week in bed. Through May and June he was back and forth between Belsize Park Gardens and Cambridge and always in ill health. So from mid-July to late September he went to Sweden and submitted himself to a health cure establishment from which he wrote voluminous letters to his brother James and to Duncan Grant. On his return to England there was a plan for Lytton to share a place outside Cambridge with Rupert Brooke (with whom his brother James was in love), but this fell through. Since his departure from Cambridge in 1905 Lytton had continued to be involved with the Apostles there and with elections to the Society of which his brother was a member. At the end of the year Strachey was again ill with intestinal problems. A life pattern of homosexual love affairs, illness, and literary reviewing carried Strachey toward his thirtieth birthday.

In July 1910 he returned to Sweden but found the health cure less beneficial than the previous year. It was following his return in September that H. A. L. Fisher proposed the book on French literature that was to lead to Strachey's breaking free of reviewing and becoming the author of more important longer studies. Strachey's interest in French

literature was mainly an interest in Racine, Voltaire, and other literature of eighteenth-century France. His mother had always admired
Voltaire, and his interest in French literature followed hers. In many
ways Strachey's rationalist, skeptical view of life derived from Voltaire
with an admixture of G. E. Moore's philosophy and a modernist angst
and insecurity provoked by reading Dostoyevski (translated by Con-
stance Garnett). Also, the ideas of Freud were beginning to be discussed by members of the Bloomsbury group, which was at its height
at this time and of which Strachey, Clive Bell, and the Stephen sisters
were principal members. However, at the end of the year Strachey
began to be involved with a new circle of friends, including Lady
Ottoline Morrell and the painter Henry Lamb, with whom he fell in
love. This was the second of the three principal homosexual romances of
Strachey's life.

The familiar pattern of Strachey's life continued into 1911. In April
he managed to restore his health with the the aid of Sanatogen and
spent eight days at Henley with Henry Lamb. On holiday with his
brother in Dorset he allowed his beard to grow; from this time on a
beard became an important part of the Strachey image. With his family
in Oxford during August he worked on his *Landmarks in French Literature* but was unable to finish it. In October he felt impelled to join
Henry Lamb who was painting in Brittany. Returning to Belsize Park
Gardens, he finished his French literature book, which was not, however, published until the new year. This book was the first full-scale
project that Strachey, at the age of thirty-one, had brought to successful completion. He had finally abandoned his work on Warren Hastings a year earlier.

The completion of the book on French literature and its successful
reception (it was praised in the *Times Literary Supplement* in an early
review) gave Strachey confidence as a writer. In a letter of 24 February
1912 to Ottoline Morrell he affirmed his wish to follow a career in
literary work. This intention he adhered to, and all three of his best-
known works—*Eminent Victorians* (1918), *Queen Victoria* (1921), and
Elizabeth and Essex (1928)—were completed during the last fifteen years
of his life.

On the last of these subjects he had already attempted to write a
tragic drama, and with his passion for Racine it was a dramatist that
Strachey wished to be. He had considerable experience of the contemporary theater from his *Spectator* reviewing and was widely read in Shake-

speare and his contemporaries. By the end of May he had completed the first two acts of a four-act drama "A Son of Heaven."

Set in China during the Boxer rebellion of 1900, "A Son of Heaven" is a tragic melodrama. Although several theater managers showed interest in it soon after its completion, it was not performed until the mid-twenties when it was given two performances to raise money for one of Philippa Strachey's feminist causes. It received a short run in London and presentation on radio after World War II but has never been published.

In September 1912, as a result of the success of *Landmarks in French Literature,* Harold Cox offered Strachey the chance to write for the *Edinburgh Review.* In the middle of October he began an article on Madame du Deffand. These longer pieces allowed him more room to develop his ideas than the short *Spectator* reviews had done. A further indication of his growing confidence and development is revealed by the fact that at the end of October he conceived the idea of producing "Victorian Silhouettes" that was to lead five years later to the publication of *Eminent Victorians.* In February–March 1913 Henry Lamb painted his famous portrait of the bearded, elongated Lytton Strachey. At the same time Strachey was completing his story *Ermyntrude and Esmeralda.* His commitment to life as a writer was now considerable.

In July 1913 a friend, Hilton Young, offered Strachey a year's tenancy of a country house in Wiltshire called The Lacket. This would allow Strachey some much-needed independence. In October he set himself up there. Prior to this, on 19 August, Virginia Woolf attempted suicide, thus provoking a reunion of the Bloomsbury friends at the Bells' establishment at Asheham.

At Christmas 1914 Strachey read *Ermyntrude and Esmeralda* to his friends at The Lacket. But England was now at war, and this was to impel Strachey toward a greater involvement in politics. His writing about the Victorian ideals and society that Strachey felt had produced the war became more satirical. "Cardinal Manning," completed at the beginning of 1915, was intended as an attack on Victorian hypocrisy and false ideology. For the next six months Strachey threw himself into the writing of his "Florence Nightingale," which exposed the horrors of war and poor military administration. The European war was raging in Belgium and France simultaneously. The death of their friend Rupert Brooke on 23 April 1915 intensified Strachey's and his brother James's sense of the futility of war.

Much of Strachey's time was now spent at Garsington, the home near Oxford of Lady Ottoline and her husband Philip Morrell, where a resistance to the war began to be organized. War hysteria was mounting in the fall of 1915. The Derby Plan leading to conscription was introduced in October. The public attitude in the country was ugly. The prosecution of D. H. Lawrence's *The Rainbow* exemplified the growing hostility to art. Strachey's relationship with Dora Carrington began in November and at the same time he was beginning the "Dr. Arnold" section of *Eminent Victorians*.

In January 1916, as World War I rolled into its third disastrous year, the Derby Plan was followed by a Military Service Bill. The No Conscription Fellowship and the National Council against Conscription were formed in response. Bertrand Russell was prominent in these organizations. Lytton Strachey followed his brother James in becoming actively involved in them. Britain's wars had never previously been fought by conscripted armies.

On 7 March Strachey appeared before a draft board in Hampstead and read a declaration of conscientious objection. He demanded his exemption from military service. It is one of Strachey's more convincing pieces of writing. The only odd thing about it is the fact that though he objected to the moral criticism of literature, his conscientious objection is naturally enough founded on moral grounds:

I have a conscious objection to assisting, by any deliberate action of mine, in carrying on the war. This objection is not based on religious belief, but upon moral considerations, at which I arrived after long and careful thought. I do not wish to assert the extremely general proposition that I should never in any circumstances, be justified in taking part in any conceivable war; to dogmatize so absolutely upon a point so abstract would appear to me to be unreasonable. At the same time, my feeling is directed not simply against the present war: I am convinced that the whole system by which it is sought to settle international disputes by force is profoundly evil; and that, so far as I am concerned, I should be doing wrong to take any active part in it.

These conclusions have crystallized in my mind since the outbreak of war. Before that time, I was principally occupied with literary and speculative matters; but, with the war, the supreme importance of international questions was forced upon my attention. My opinions in general have been for many years strongly critical of the whole structure of society; and after a study of the diplomatic situation, and of the literature, both controversial and philosophical, arising out of the war, they developed naturally with those which I now hold. My convictions as to my duty with regard to the war, have not been formed either rashly or lightly; and I shall not act against those convictions, whatever the consequences may be.

This was the occasion on which Strachey made his famous reply when asked the standard question by the Tribunal, "What would you do if you saw a German soldier trying to rape your sister?" by saying, "I should attempt to come—between them."[12]

The conscription issue was intense at this time. In April one conscientious objector, Ernest Everett, was sentenced to two months hard labor while Bertrand Russell was fined one hundred pounds for one of the tracts he wrote for the No Conscription Fellowship. Strachey, however, after a medical examination, was given a complete exemption from military service on medical grounds.

In June Strachey stayed at Wisset Lodge in Suffolk where his friends Duncan Grant and David Garnett were officially registered as farmers under the National Service Act. A piece he wrote at this time called "June 16, 1916" (*SP*, 139–56), detailing a day in his life, expresses his response to his experience, a life largely governed, it seems, by his homosexual compulsion. During the second fortnight of August he was on holiday with Dora Carrington in Wales. From there they went on to spend a few days in Bath. It was at this time that they began to consider living together. Strachey was thirty-six and Carrington in her early twenties. In October he managed to get his "Dr. Arnold" essay finished and began work on "General Gordon," the final portrait of *Eminent Victorians*.

While staying with Dorelia John (wife of the painter Augustus John) at Alderney Manor, Parkstone, Strachey invited Carrington to join him. Her relationship with Mark Gertler came to an end in April. At the end of May Strachey had to undergo another army medical. He was classified as category 4 with the request to report to the board every six months. With much gadding about between Garsington and Cambridge, sometimes accompanied by Carrington, his work on General Gordon was interrupted. However, he managed to complete it by the end of August when he read various sections of *Eminent Victorians* to his friends the Woolfs and the Bells.

At the end of October 1917, Carrington found The Mill House, Tidmarsh, in Berkshire, where Strachey was to spend the happiest, most stable, and most successful years of his writing life. In November he sent the manuscript of *Eminent Victorians* to Chatto and Windus and in December learned that it had been accepted for publication. At

Christmas Strachey arrived at Tidmarsh where he began reading Queen Victoria's letters.

Published early in 1918, *Eminent Victorians* was a great success. Although it drew Strachey into controversy with Edmund Gosse, the book was favorably reviewed and even recommended by Prime Minister Asquith in a lecture he gave at Oxford. With the Great War lurching to a conclusion, people were ready to turn their backs upon the Victorian era that Strachey so mercilessly satirized. This is the explanation generally offered for the popular success of *Eminent Victorians,* the book that made Bertrand Russell laugh aloud in his prison cell where he was serving a sentence for his antiwar activities.

Strachey became a celebrity on the strength of *Eminent Victorians.* He was invited to visit the Duchess of Marlborough, received an invitation from the prime minister and also from Edward Hudson, the proprietor of *Country Life,* to his house in Northumberland. Strachey had become a lion of the literary world.

In August Ralph Partridge arrived at Tidmarsh. For several years he, Strachey, and Carrington were to live happily together at Tidmarsh in what has been called "a bi-sexual *ménage à trois.*"[13] Strachey was thirty-eight years old. His life seemed settled, perhaps for the first time. The agitations of youth were past, and Strachey could feel, at last, that he had accomplished something significant—an arraignment of the Victorian society in which he had grown up, whose values he had rejected because he felt that they had produced the Great War with its terrible devastation of human life.

Strachey was now a writer whose work was much in request. Middleton Murry, for example, wanted him to write for the *Athenaeum* and, after visiting Tidmarsh, took back with him "Lady Hester Stanhope," which is certainly a piece of biographical rather than literary critical writing.

Through the spring and summer of 1919 Strachey was making frequent visits to the British Museum to do his research for the biography of Queen Victoria. Visiting Garsington in May, he met T. S. Eliot and in June and July received two invitations to the Asquiths. The shy, lanky, red-bearded recluse had now become a socialite making quips in a high voice and intimate conversation in a low one. At the end of September he returned to Tidmarsh to spend a quiet six months' work.

In April 1920 Strachey, Ralph, and Carrington set out on a trip to Spain that was eventually to prove disastrous as far as the harmony of the "bi-sexual *ménage à trois*" was concerned, for Carrington was to become romantically involved with Gerald Brenan, who they visited at Yegen. When revealed, this provoked the jealousy of Ralph Partridge and relations between Ralph and Carrington were never the same after this. Then, Ralph became involved with Frances Marshall and spent less and less time with Strachey and Carrington.

Strachey's life pattern was now one of winter work and summer visiting. When Ralph and Carrington made a trial marriage in October, they spent a week together in London. In essence, the dynamics of the *ménage à trois* were that Strachey was attracted to Ralph, Carrington to Strachey, and Ralph to Carrington. It was a delicate balance that took all of Strachey's diplomacy to maintain. Carrington and, more particularly, Strachey were somewhat incompetent in practical affairs, although Carrington was an accomplished cook, painter, gardener, and craftswoman. They relied on Ralph to take care of many of their concerns. Strachey, for example, bought a car on the strength of the proceeds from his books; Ralph drove the car. Ralph would always take care of their travel arrangements for journeys on which Strachey would travel first-class while Ralph and Carrington traveled third class.[14]

In October 1920 Strachey returned from his September visits to finish *Queen Victoria* at Tidmarsh. The book, which his mother had counseled him against writing, suggesting instead he write about Disraeli, proved to be as successful as *Eminent Victorians,* if not more so. Here Strachey, perhaps more sensitive to his mother's concern, compromised—Victoria and Albert were treated with, at worst, comedy whereas the subjects of *Eminent Victorians* had been satirized. Besides, Strachey aware, perhaps, of charges of unscholarly imputation, if not downright distortion, in *Eminent Victorians* provided a proper system of reference in *Queen Victoria.* The result was a more objective and scholarly piece of work. In its balanced assessment of its subject, it is Strachey's most mature work. *Eminent Victorians* is the product of a young man's angry contempt for Victorian hypocrisy, *Queen Victoria* more the product of a man, accepted by the literary world, who seeks to consolidate his reputation.

On the completion of *Queen Victoria,* Strachey spent some time at his family's new home at 51 Gordon Square, Bloomsbury. From there he made periodic weekend visits to Cambridge and Tidmarsh. In May he set out with his sister Philippa to visit their friends the Berensons in Florence. In the middle of the month he learned of a crisis in the relations between Ralph and Carrington who were married on 21 May. They, then, set out for a honeymoon in Venice where they joined Strachey and Philippa at the end of the month.

In October Strachey and his Bloomsbury friends became involved in the Dr. Oscar Levy affair and opposed Levy's expulsion from England. Levy, who had left Britain in 1914, returned in 1920. Although he had relinquished his German citizenship, he was deported to France under the Aliens Restriction Act.[15] Strachey spent the winter of 1922 at Tidmarsh and Gordon Square. In February Carrington and Ralph traveled to Vienna where Alix (James Strachey's wife) was suffering from pleurisy. She and James had been studying with Sigmund Freud. They were responsible for the deepened interest in psychology that is present in *Elizabeth and Essex*.

In June 1922 Strachey bought a car (to be driven by Ralph), and after visiting Venice with Sebastian Sprott, he sublet Tidmarsh in August. He, Carrington, and Ralph made a motor tour through Devon and Wales. Following his customary autumn visits, Strachey accompanied his brother James to a conference on psychoanalysis in Berlin where Freud was making a presentation. In October he returned to Tidmarsh where the Partridges seemed to have reached an accord in their relationship.

After visiting Garsington in February 1923, Strachey went to Gordon Square to be with his mother who was now eighty-three and virtually blind. At the end of March he traveled with Ralph and Carrington to North Africa from where he sent his essay on Sarah Bernhardt (in which he commends her performance in Racine's *Phèdre*) to Keynes for publication in the *Nation and Athenaeum*. In the middle of April the three left Tunis for Palermo, Naples, and Rome, and arrived back in London at the end of May. Strachey was now living the life of a successful author—no longer working even in the winter.

Strachey was entering middle age. July was spent with weekends at Blenheim and Tidmarsh, while in August he toured France with Ralph and Carrington. In November Ralph met Frances Marshall; this was the beginning of the end of the Ralph-Carrington marriage. It took all Strachey's diplomacy to hold them together for the remaining years of his life.

January 1924 marked another turning point in Strachey's life. After a few days in Paris at the beginning of the year, he returned and bought Ham Spray House in Berkshire where he spent the last six years of his life. Through March, Ralph was looking after both Strachey and Carrington. In April Strachey convalesced with his sister at Lyme Regis. In May Gerald Brenan came to London, and Carrington visited him there and entertained him at Tidmarsh—now with Ralph's blessing. Ralph's new relationship with Frances Marshall diminished his attachment to Carrington. In the end Strachey would have to ask Ralph to give Carrington and himself a little more of his time at Ham Spray. On 15 July Strachey left Tidmarsh; it was a sad departure. Later, installed at Ham Spray House, he would weep while listening to Schubert on the gramophone when he was reminded of the happiness of his six years at Tidmarsh, the most peaceful and productive years of his life.

In 1925 Strachey's literary success was confirmed by the invitation he received to deliver the annual Leslie Stephen Lecture at Cambridge in June. The subject he chose was Alexander Pope, and it was in this lecture that he presented the image of Pope as the hateful monkey dropping ladles of boiling oil on his victims, an image that lovers of Pope have resented ever since. The lecture was, in fact, fully in praise of Pope, who Strachey had always admired and had more than once written about during his days as a reviewer. In the lecture he tried again to attack Matthew Arnold's view of literature as a criticism of life, suggesting that the heroic couplet itself was Pope's criticism of life.

On 12 July the first performance of Strachey's "A Son of Heaven" took place. Although Strachey was involved in the lead up to this largely amateur production, particularly in attempting to sort out rows between the director and the leading lady, he did not stay in London to witness the performances but set off to the Dolomites for a holiday with Sebastian Sprott.

In October 1925 Ralph Partridge left Ham Spray to live in London with Frances Marshall and only returned for visits on weekends. This was a kind of *de facto* confirmation of the "marriage" between Carrington and Strachey though both, of course, had other affairs. The complication of their emotional lives produced considerable pain and tension for both, though not necessarily between each other. Carrington found Strachey the only person she could really talk to who did not judge her.

At the end of the year Strachey began work on *Elizabeth and Essex.* Apart from his miniature portraits of historians, it was his last venture and he certainly tried to make it his best. As will be discussed later, he tried, in *Elizabeth and Essex,* to bring together all the threads of his career as a writer. He revived an early work, *Essex: A Tragedy,* and tried, in effect, to produce a tragic drama drawing upon his interest both in Shakespeare and Racine. He also tried to enrich his writing

with poetic imagery as can be seen in his handling of the fire and
serpent images in the book. More important, he attempted to deepen
the psychological exploration, particularly of the character of Elizabeth,
through the use of Freudian psychology learned from his brother James
and sister-in-law Alix. But more important yet, he expressed his own
compulsions in his writing, dramatizing himself, as J. M. Keynes
noticed,[16] as both Elizabeth and Essex. In many respects the "tragedy"
is a work of fiction.[17] For a writer who found difficulty, as Gabriel
Merle has noted,[18] in bringing his affective life into his writing, *Elizabeth and Essex* is the place where this occurs, where we find Strachey the
man most fully *in* his writing. Not surprisingly, the book proved an
agony to write, and the writing followed the contours of his final,
unhappy homosexual affair with Roger Senhouse.

This liaison, which was to last until the end of his life, began in
August 1926. Although Strachey suffered from migraines and fever in
November, he was well enough to take a fortnight's holiday with Roger
Senhouse in Rome at the end of this year. In January 1927 he returned
to Ham Spray and completed his biographical essay on "Dr. North."
He rarely left Ham Spray from January until May. The pattern of
winter work appeared to be returning, yet his progress on *Elizabeth and
Essex* was very slow.

In London in June he met the biographer Emil Ludwig whose work
he is thought to have influenced. In July, while Carrington took a two-
week holiday with James and Alix Strachey in Munich, Sebastian
Sprott stayed with Strachey and helped to put Strachey's voluminous
correspondence in order. In September Strachey worked on his "portraits in miniature" of Carlyle and Gibbon as well as writing a review
article on a biography of Edward VII for the *Daily Mail*.

During the autumn he worked hard on *Elizabeth and Essex* but spent
weekends at Cambridge with the Lucases and at Brighton with Roger
Senhouse. On 2 November, he finished his portrait of Gibbon, and on
the 13th he received a telegram from Allen and Unwin inviting him to
edit the Greville Memoirs. Frances and Ralph, Stephen and Julia
Tomlin, and Strachey's brother James were at Ham Spray for Christmas. At the end of December Strachey returned to work on *Elizabeth
and Essex,* which he completed in April 1928.

Since improvements were in progress at Ham Spray when he returned from vacation in August, Strachey went to London where he
met Lady Ottoline Morrell, W. B. Yeats, and Aldous Huxley. He
worked on his planned edition of the Greville Memoirs at the British

Museum during September. In October he returned to Ham Spray, and in November involved Ralph and Frances in the editing of the Greville Memoirs at the British Museum. This work was not published until several years after Strachey's death. On 15 December Lady Jane Maria Strachey died in her eighty-eighth year, a much sharper loss to Strachey than the loss of his father had been.

Work on the Greville Memoirs was progressing well in January 1929, and Strachey was at work on his miniature portrait of the historian Creighton for Desmond MacCarthy's *Life and Letters* series. In May he met the novelist Richard Hughes and visited Cambridge, Bath, and London for theater and dinner engagements in May and June. Perhaps prompted by his mother's death the previous December or by a sense of the brevity of his own life, he made his will on 13 June: his books were to go to Roger Senhouse, his papers to his brother James, and Ham Spray to Carrington and Ralph. In July he spent a fortnight in Holland with Carrington, Ralph, and Sebastian Sprott. On his return he discovered that Roger Senhouse had left for France with a friend. This was a blow to Strachey's third and final sustained homosexual liaison.

An exhibition of D. H. Lawrence's paintings opened in London on 15 July. When the paintings were seized by the police, Strachey was one of the signatories of a protest petition. Throughout his life he was opposed to censorship. In August he continued work on the Greville Memoirs, while his brother-in-law Stephen Tomlin made a bust of him. The poor health that had dogged Strachey throughout his life seemed to be pressing in on him as he approached his fiftieth birthday.

In the middle of January 1931 Strachey returned to Ham Spray. He seemed to have a premonition that not much time was left him because on 20 March he had a long conversation with Carrington on the subject of death. In July "Mopsa" the pen name Carrington used, won first prize in a *Week-end Review* contest with a parodic obituary of Strachey. Strachey was at Cambridge at the time and sent her a congratulatory telegram. Carrington, however, suffered agonies of guilt over what she had done, especially during Strachey's final illness. She, in fact, convinced herself that she had willed his death and this, in part, led to her suicide. In August Strachey began the essay on *Othello* which remained unfinished at the time of his death. It was intended to be the first of a series of essays on Shakespeare.

On 3 September Strachey set out on his own to visit Paris, Reims, Nancy, and Strasbourg, and returned to England via Paris. It was the last of his many visits to France. He recorded it in a diary that is one of

his last pieces of writing (*SP*, 160–84). Back from France, he spent a
weekend with Roger Senhouse in Brighton in October. In November
Aldous and Maria Huxley spent a weekend with him at Ham Spray. In
the same month, however, he became ill during a dinner in London
with Clive Bell. He returned to Ham Spray and from the end of
November was never able to get out of bed again. At first his niece Dr.
Elinor Rendel diagnosed typhoid but, when he failed to respond to
treatment, Sir Maurice Cassidy was called in. He diagnosed colitis with
an ulcer. Professor Leonard Dudgeon and the surgeon Dr. John Ryle
were also consulted during December. Strachey, however, failed to
respond to treatment. His relations and friends rallied round him and
his sisters nursed him lovingly. He suffered bravely, at one point
observing "If this is death, I don't think much of it." On 20 January his
condition worsened, after what had looked like an improvement. On
the same day he declared that he had always wished to marry Carrington. Carrington, who had agonized through Strachey's illness, tried to
commit suicide that night. Strachey died at 1:30 P.M. on 21 January.
His brother James insisted upon a post mortem, and it was discovered
that he had all along been suffering from stomach cancer. He was
cremated in London and his ashes placed in the family chapel in Somerset near the family seat, Sutton Court.

During his last days he wrote several religious poems, which his
biographer Michael Holroyd quotes. The last one is as follows:

> Insensibly I turn, I glide
> A little nearer to thy side . . .
> At last! Ah, Lord, the joy, the peace,
> The triumph and the sweet release,
> When, after all the wandering pain,
> The separation, long and vain,
> Into the field, the sea, the sun,
> Thy culminating hands, I come![19]

It seems likely that primarily Lytton Strachey will be remembered
for his work as a biographer. His literary criticism is at its best in the
tradition of Edwardian belletristic impressionism, although his work
on behalf of Racine constitutes a genuine contribution to criticism. As
his career advanced, Strachey wrote less and less literary criticism and
more and more biography.

As a biographer he is chiefly notable for spearheading what has been
called the "new biography." With *Eminent Victorians* he initiated a

movement away from the standard Victorian two-volume biography that was usually panegyric. *Eminent Victorians* was sharply critical of its subjects, so much so that many will question the degree of deception practiced there. *Queen Victoria* is a more responsible piece of biography. Where *Eminent Victorians* enjoyed a *succès de scandale*, *Queen Victoria* ensured Strachey's acceptance by the social as well as the literary world. In *Elizabeth and Essex* Strachey took his interest in psychoanalytical biography further. He also sought in that book to fulfill his desire to be a poet and tragic dramatist.

Although Strachey was born into the English upper middle-class and enjoyed considerable success as a writer, his life, despite his rounds of European travel and visiting, was not a happy one. His homosexuality, which he justified by appeals to Plato, Shakespeare, and even Jesus Christ, at times provided him with heights of identification with such lovers as Duncan Grant, Henry Lamb, and Roger Senhouse, but it also brought him anguish. As early as his Liverpool diary he spoke of his emotional life as a "tragedy."

Gabriel Merle, at the end of a two-volume, nearly one-thousand-page study of Strachey, places him in the literary pantheon somewhere between Horace Walpole and Charles Lamb,[20] which suggests that Strachey is a minor writer. Merle's judgment would seem to emphasize the letter writer (although little of Strachey's voluminous correspondence has yet been published) and the essayist. Recently Michael Holroyd and Paul Levy have argued that Strachey's greatest success is precisely as an essay writer.[21]

Although one may agree with F. R. Leavis's judgment that Strachey is essentially lightweight and that it is remarkable that he was ever taken as seriously as he was,[22] Strachey's writing does remind us in the later twentieth century of something, and that is, precisely, Dr. Johnson's common reader. At a time when academic English produces postmodernist work that the common reader could never (nor should he) be expected to understand, Strachey's writing in its general accessibility reminds us of a literary culture in which most intelligent readers can participate together. Strachey, who was in many ways a self-consciously intellectual and even intellectually snobbish man, never produced a piece of published writing that an ordinary literate person could not understand. Depending upon our attitude toward the Victorians, Strachey's *Eminent Victorians* provokes mirth or angry retorts, yet its readability, like that of *Queen Victoria* and *Elizabeth and Essex,* is hard to deny. He shook up biography when it needed shaking up; he was the kind of irritant who provoked a necessary change.

Chapter Two

The Literary Critic: Early Essays, Reviews, and *Landmarks in French Literature* (1912)

Early Essays, Reviews

Strachey's first book, *Landmarks in French Literature*, was published in 1912 when he was thirty-two years old. It was by no means his first work as a writer. Indeed, it was preceded by nearly ten years of literary apprenticeship and, in fact, by a whole life of writing. Strachey wrote poetry from an early age, and very early letters to his younger brother can be read in the British Library. Michael Holroyd's *Lytton Strachey By Himself* (1971) contains the early diary that Strachey kept at the age of twelve of his journey to the Mediterranean and through the Suez Canal to the Cape of Good Hope. Besides, there was a considerable amount of letter and essay writing at school and at Liverpool University College.

As a student at Cambridge, Strachey published poetry in the *Cambridge Review* in 1901 and 1902, which was reprinted in a volume called *Euphrosyne: A Collection of Verse* that he published with fellow students. In 1902 he won the Chancellor's Gold Medal for "Ely: An Ode," which he recited in the Senate House on 10 June and which was published in *Proclusionae Academicae* by the university press in the same year. In Appendix 2 of his two-volume study of Strachey, Gabriel Merle lists twenty-three essays that Strachey read to the Midnight Society, the Sunday Essay Society, and the Apostles at Cambridge between 1900 and 1912. Several of these essays (written to be read and hence helping to shape Strachey's conversational prose style) have been collected by Paul Levy in his volume *The Really Interesting Question* (1972). This volume also contains conversations and short stories that Strachey wrote at this time. Besides, he tried his hand at drama, writing *Essex: A Tragedy*, which he later drew upon in *Elizabeth and Essex*. He also completed a tragic melodrama, "A Son of Heaven," set in China at the time of the Boxer Rebellion, but this was not produced until 1925.

There was, too, his historical work on Warren Hastings submitted initially for the Greaves prize in 1901 and then in extended form in the hope of obtaining a fellowship at Trinity College, Cambridge, in 1904 and 1905. In 1905 he submitted a twenty-thousand-word essay on English Letter Writers for the Le Bas Prize at Cambridge.

The real apprenticeship began in 1904, after Strachey had completed his degree in history, when he began to write articles and reviews for the *Independent Review* and for his cousin St. Loe Strachey's the *Spectator*. Indeed, in the eight-year period between January 1904, when he published his first review in the *Spectator*, and January 1912, when *Landmarks in French Literature* appeared, Strachey published over eighty reviews in the *Spectator*. During 1908, for example, he was publishing weekly reviews for his cousin's periodical. Thirty-five of these reviews were selected by Strachey's brother James and published as *Spectatorial Essays* in 1964. It would be hard to imagine a better apprenticeship for a critic and biographer. Gabriel Merle divides Strachey's career in just this way. The division is, perhaps, too stringent, but it offers a fine insight into Strachey's development as a writer. Until the publication of *Landmarks in French Literature*, Strachey was writing primarily literary criticism and thereafter biography, but the two strands were intertwined, as will be seen.

Before discussing Strachey's method as a critic it is useful to indicate briefly the nature and range of his critical writing between 1904 and 1912. He reviewed books on English and French literature and eventually became the *Spectator*'s drama critic. He also wrote on historical and biographical topics. For Strachey, educated in history at Cambridge but having also studied literature at Liverpool University College, the reviewing work for the *Spectator* provided a further background in English and French literature from which he could undertake a book like *Landmarks in French Literature* for the Home University Library when invited to do so by H. A. L. Fisher in September 1910. This book, which he completed in about a year, was, in effect, the culmination of six years of literary apprenticeship during which he wrote hundreds of letters and poems as well as nearly a hundred published reviews. The majority of these reviews concerned English rather than French literature. They were written under the *Spectator*'s constraints of space and his cousin St. Loe's strong editorial hand. Strachey must have been pleased when opportunities arose to produce longer pieces like "Shakespeare's Final Period" for the *Independent Review* in August 1906, his essay on Lady Mary Wortley Montagu for the *Albany Review* in September 1907, and "The Last Elizabethan" on Thomas Lovell Beddoes in the *New Quarterly* in June 1908. These, not surprisingly, emerged as his best pieces of criticism. Naturally, he selected them for inclusion in his *Books and Characters* (1922), the volume that contains his own choice of the best of his early pieces. It contains no *Spectator* reviews.

Other opportunities for more sustained writing arose in these early years as when the London publisher Henry Frowde gave Strachey the chance to provide an introduction to a new edition of Elizabeth Inchbald's *A Simple Story*. Here one can see Strachey at work as both critic and biographer. Another longer piece called "The Rousseau Affair" appeared in the *New Quarterly* in May 1910. In the light of *Landmarks in French Literature*, it is interesting that two of the more sustained pieces written in the apprenticeship period should have concerned French subjects, especially since, of the ninety-eight *Spectator* reviews written between 1904 and 1912, eighty-three concerned topics relating to English and only nine topics relating to French literature. Several other pieces on French literature were written for other periodicals such as the *Independent Review* and the *Speaker,* but on the whole this count would seem to confirm Gabriel Merle's argument that Strachey was hardly overqualified when commissioned to write *Landmarks in French Literature.* Indeed, as a history student who had become a student of English literature in the mill of literary reviewing, Strachey would have been better qualified to attempt a *Landmarks in English Literature.*

But what kind of literary reviewer and critic was Lytton Strachey, particularly in these early days? One sees him at this time primarily as a reviewer of books of or about English literature and drama, or flexing his muscles in longer pieces like the essays on Racine and Thomas Lovell Beddoes, both of which he chose to preserve in *Books and Characters* (1922). In fairness to Strachey it would be best to focus critical attention on pieces like the latter. Nevertheless, it is true to say that no very serious claims can be made for Lytton Strachey as a literary critic. It is for his contributions to the changing art of biography that he is best remembered. As a literary critic, he writes in the post-Swinburnian, pre-New Critical style somewhat in the manner of Edmund Gosse and Sir Walter Raleigh. Without the addition of his biographical work, his reputation would not extend beyond theirs.

This means that Strachey's literary criticism shows little rigor of close analysis. He is happy enough, like his late Victorian and Edwardian-Georgian contemporaries, to flit from literary flower to flower speaking of beauty and truth, though at times words like "presentment," "reality," and "vitality" appear. Serious argument and judgment can be found in pieces like the "Shakespeare's Final Period" essay of 1906 that was also collected in *Books and Characters* (1922) and in the Racine and Beddoes essays. Of these the argument about Shakespeare being bitter rather than reconciliatory and serene in his final period is wrong, though interestingly wrong. The case for Beddoes is overargued, for in the end Beddoes's Elizabethanism is Elizabethan pastiche. Indeed, Beddoes is more like a last romantic than a last Elizabethan. The Racine essay constitutes Strachey's most serious claim for attention as a literary critic. As *Landmarks in French Literature* has a place though a minor one, in the study of French literature, Strachey's work must have a place in Racine's English rehabilitation.

Strachey's literary criticism finally founders on the rock of critical judgment. His attack on Matthew Arnold in the *New Statesman* in August 1914, "A Victorian Critic," ironically brought to a close Strachey's work as a critic. He was unable to accept Arnold's view of literature as a criticism of life. As a biographer, Strachey could criticize life, but he could not accept such a critical examination of literature. For Strachey, literature was expression, art, form; it had, in his view, no moral purpose or intention. It is significant that this restricted view of literature incapacitated him not only as a literary critic but also as an imaginative writer. He could exercise his moral sense in writing biography, but apparently not in writing literature or literary criticism, in which the very word *criticism* expresses the need for an act of judgment. Thus, though Strachey could turn out heroic couplets with ease, he failed to produce a body of significant poetry; though he tried his hand at fiction, his work has enjoyed little success after posthumous publication. Although he wished to play the tragedian to Keynes's economist and join Duncan Grant as a great artist as well as a great friend, his obsession with people and his suspicion of art and literature as a mere bag of tricks led Strachey finally to biography and away from literature and criticism.

A consideration of selected examples of Strachey's critical and biographical writing up to and including *Landmarks in French Literature* helps in understanding his methods and placing his literary and critical ideals. "English Letter Writers" (1905), which he wrote for the Le Bas Prize at Cambridge, remained unpublished in his lifetime, but was collected by his brother James in *Characters and Commentaries* (1933). It is Strachey's earliest attempt at a sustained piece of critical writing. In

its length (twenty thousand words) and chronological approach to its
subject, it is almost a short book and in this respect anticipates *Landmarks in French Literature*. It is even divided into six chapters. "English
Letter Writers" allows us to see Strachey's sense of the development of
English literary history, for it covers the period from the Elizabethans
to the nineteenth century. He himself was most interested in the
Elizabethan and eighteenth-century periods in English literature.

Strachey characterizes letters in a manner that reveals the Voltairean
staple of his own literary style. Like Voltaire, Strachey always employs
antithesis and the balanced sentence. "The most lasting utterances of a
man are his studied writings; the least are his conversations. His letters
hover midway between these two extremes; and the fate which is reserved for them is capable of infinite gradations, from instant annihila-
tion up to immortality."[1] A divided nature seeking balance is revealed
in the very tissue of Strachey's style, as can be seen here. Although he
was later to attempt to eschew morality in literature, in 1905 he was
aware of the essential relation between literature and morality. Significantly, he sees this relation as part of the relation between life and
literature that Arnold desiderates:

The crisis of the Reformation had shaken the whole fabric of established
thought. Everywhere questions were rising up which had long lain entranced
beneath the spell of mother Church; and of these questions none were more
important and pressing than the moral ones. The letters of the time show how
eagerly men were feeling their way towards the reconstitution of an ethical
code. (*CC*, 5)

As Strachey recognizes, this was the age that produced, besides the
King James Bible, the poetry of Shakespeare and the prose of Bacon. In
noticing the gulf that exists between Elizabethan and late seventeenth-
century letter writing, Strachey is observing what T. S. Eliot was later
to characterize as the "dissociation of sensibility," but in his predilection for enlightenment and progress Strachey fails to draw the conclusions that Eliot does. Strachey writes, "the chief end of stylistic art has
come to be the appearance of colloquial easiness. The change has not
been without its drawbacks; there has been a loss of profundity, of
seriousness, of grandeur" (*CC*, 9). However, Strachey does not stop
there, but continues, "But there have been corresponding gains—in
lightness of touch, in clarity, and in play of personal feeling. The old
style of letter is the more instructive; the new is the more entertaining"

(*CC*,9). The final, balanced antithesis points toward the narrowly aesthetic estimate of literature that Strachey was to espouse by 1914.

Strachey's admiration for the eighteenth century is given full expression at the opening of his second chapter. This taste, fully formed by the age of twenty-five, remained with Strachey for life and is symbolized by the portrait of Voltaire that hung over his study fire in his later years. The passage is a representative piece of Strachey's generalized, belletristic writing, the kind of writing that makes it more accurate to characterize Strachey as "a man of letters" than as a literary critic:

In the troubled sea of History two epochs seem to stand out like enchanted islands of delight and repose—the Age of the Antonines and the eighteenth century. Gibbon's splendid eulogy of "that period in the history of the world which elapsed from the death of Domitian to the accession of Commodus" suggests at once to our minds the rival glories of his own epoch. Who does not feel that the polished pomp of Gibbon's sentences is the true offspring of the age of Handel and of Reynolds, and yet it might have been composed as fittingly amid the elaborate colonnades and the Corinthian grandeur of the villa of Adrianus? (*CC*, 11)

Like Swift, Voltaire, and Horace Walpole, Gibbon was an eighteenth-century figure who Strachey admired, as will be seen in his treatment of six historians in *Portraits in Miniature*. But Strachey's attraction to the artificial stands revealed in the alliterative "polished pomp of Gibbon's sentences." In answer to Strachey's question, another can be asked, who does not feel the insincerity and affectation of "polished pomp"? This predilection for "polished pomp" is what draws Strachey to Horace Walpole and leads him to make the claim for Walpole's letters that "these famous letters" have "a position of preeminence unrivalled in English literature, and only paralleled by the letters of Voltaire in the literature of the world" (*CC*,32). He praises Lady Mary Wortley Montagu and Thomas Gray, yet condemns Lord Chesterfield and William Cowper as letter writers. The study fizzles out in the early nineteenth century after Strachey has compared the movement from the eighteenth century to the romantic period to the change from a smooth flowing river to the sea. Two accounts of executions, one by Walpole and the other by Byron, are compared, but Strachey seems to miss the irony of his own sentence: "The careful elegance of the eighteenth century was utterly alien to Byron's manner of writing" (*CC*,56).

From a critic of English literature one would naturally expect a continuous engagement with Shakespeare. "Shakespeare's Final Period," which appeared in the *Independent Review* in 1906 and was collected in *Books and Characters* (1922), is probably Strachey's best piece of writing about Shakespeare even though it was his first. It was originally presented to the Sunday Essay Society on 29 November 1903. "Shakespeare's Final Period" is a challenge to the general view that the later plays reveal Shakespeare in a post-tragic mood of reconciliation. Strachey's argument that the late plays reveal bitterness and disillusionment on Shakespeare's part has the quality of devil's advocacy about it, but a devil's advocacy that is sufficiently intelligent to deserve attention. That one comes away from the argument convinced that the general view holds, does not detract from the fact that Strachey challenges his reader to think afresh about Shakespeare's late plays.

Strachey focuses on the end of Shakespeare's life in a way that anticipates the deathbed set pieces that he includes in so many of his biographical studies:

For some reason or another, the end of a man's life seems naturally to afford the light by which the rest of it should be read; last thoughts do appear in some strange way to be really best and truest; and this is particularly the case when they fit nicely with the rest of the story, and are, perhaps, just what one likes to think oneself.[2]

Although the reader might agree with Strachey that not all is sunny in Shakespeare's last plays, it is impossible to concede that in them Shakespeare is "getting bored . . . bored, in fact, with everything except poetry and poetical dreams" (*BC*,64). Indeed, what the reader encounters here is Strachey transferring his own boredom onto Shakespeare, just as in his Liverpool diary (1897) he attributed a disgust and cynicism to Shakespeare that he felt with himself.

In order to make his point about Shakespeare's disillusionment in the later plays, Strachey compares *A Midsummer Night's Dream* and *The Tempest*. He concludes by quoting Caliban's, "You taught me language, and my profit on't / Is, I know how to curse" and raises the question "Is this Caliban addressing Prospero, or Job addressing God? It may be either; but it is not serene, nor benign, nor pastoral, nor 'On the Heights' " (*BC*,69). But surely here Shakespeare must be taken on his own terms. Caliban is addressing Miranda, and to view the play from Caliban's point of view is devil's advocacy run mad.

That biographical and critical interests are intertwined from the beginning in Strachey's case is revealed by the essay, "Mademoiselle de Lespinasse," another of the longer pieces that first appeared in the *Independent Review* in 1906 and was later collected in *Characters and Commentaries* (1933). The essay is of interest because it reveals that Strachey was able to express more of himself in his biographical than in his critical writing. This is, perhaps, another reason why he became a biographer and largely gave up literary criticism. The essay concerns a biography of Julie de Lespinasse, who was born in Lyons on 9 November 1732 and whose letters Strachey describes as providing "the most complete analysis the world possesses of a passion which actually existed in a human mind" (*CC*, 100). Strachey himself at the time of writing the essay was involved deeply in expressing his own passion in letters, hence he naturally identifies with Julie de Lespinasse.

The biography by the Marquis de Segur that Strachey is considering in the essay presents the case that Julie de Lespinasse was the daughter of the Comte de Vichy, the eldest brother of Madame du Deffand. After discussing in this essay the hopeless passion of Julie de Lespinasse for the Marquis de Mora and then for the Comte de Guibert, Strachey went on in subsequent essays on Madame du Deffand (1913) and Mary Berry (1925) to discuss Madame du Deffand's hopeless passion for Horace Walpole and then Walpole's passion for Mary Berry. This suggests a lifelong interest in the subject of hopeless passion which surfaces first in the essay on Julie de Lespinasse. There can be little doubt that this was a deeply personal interest as Strachey was in the midst of his love affair with Duncan Grant at the time of writing this essay.

Strachey tells how Madame du Deffand brought her niece Julie out of provincial obscurity into the social glitter of her Paris salon, but the niece eventually broke with her aunt in a rift involving the *Encylopédistes* that ended the eminence of Madame du Deffand's salon. Julie's history then and subsequently was a tragic one of unhappy love affairs, first with the Spanish Marquis de Mora who died, and then with the Comte de Guibert whose indifference led to Julie's own death.

Melodramatically, Strachey writes of Julie's relation with Guibert: "Every knock upon the door brought desire and terror to her heart. The postman was a minister of death" (*CC*, 111). But it is a melodrama in which Strachey himself shares as one follows the course, for example, of his correspondence with Duncan Grant that is contemporary with this essay.[3] In all three essays of 1906, 1907, and 1925 human love is seen as an affliction. Unfortunately, throughout his life, Strachey appears to have experienced love as hopeless passion, as moments of guilty plea-

Beddoes, in fact, been a strong man he might have stood a better chance of becoming the major poet and dramatist that Strachey mistakenly took him to be.

Strachey's "Racine" essay collected in *Books and Characters* (1921), began as an essay in the *New Quarterly* (June 1908) called "The Poetry of Racine." Apart from his lifelong interest in Voltaire, Racine is the French writer about whom Strachey produced his best literary criticism. His effort to strengthen Racine's reputation with British readers was an enterprise completed and well worth Strachey's effort.

As he frequently does, Strachey begins the essay with a question. "But . . . how does it happen that while on one side of that 'span of waters' Racine is despised and Shakespeare is worshipped, on the other, Shakespeare is tolerated and Racine is adored?" (*BC,* 4) Strachey's wording is more than usually deliberate here. His intention in the essay is to persuade his English audience to, at least, "tolerate" rather than "despise" Racine. Strachey is more convincing when he begins with a question, as he does here, than when he starts with an exaggerated claim of the kind he makes in the Beddoes essay. Strachey proceeds by illustrating the breadth of the gap over Racine that exists in the work of English and French critics by citing the views of John Bailey in *The Claims of French Poetry* (a book that Strachey reviewed for the *Spectator*) and M. Lemaitre.

Strachey wishes to elicit sympathy for Racine and states that "it is obvious that no poet can be admired or understood by those who quarrel with the whole fabric of his writing and condemn the very principles of his art" (*BC,* 7). He goes on to suggest that Racine should claim our consideration on the grounds that his influence has prevailed in modern drama in ways that Shakespeare's has not. He argues that "The method of *Macbeth* has been, as it were, absorbed by that of the modern novel; the method of *Britannicus* still rules the stage" (*BC,* 9–10). This accords, at least, with the view that the strength of Elizabethan drama was present in English literature more in the Victorian novel than in Victorian drama or poetry. Racine's attention, Strachey claims, is fixed on "spiritual crisis"; he seeks to enhance "the effect of the inner tragedy" (*BC,* 10).

Because of their love of Shakespeare, Strachey claims that English audiences have an ingrained preference for excess: "our own literature is one in which rarity of style, pushed often to the verge of extravagance, reigns supreme" (*BC,* 13). Strachey's love of Voltaire and the eighteenth century emerges in this depiction of English taste:

. . . in Shakespeare, with whom expression is stretched to the bursting point, the national style finds at once its consummate example and its final justification. But the result is that we have grown so unused to other kinds of poetical beauty, that we have now come to believe, with Mr. Bailey, that poetry apart from "le mot rare," is an impossibility. The beauties of restraint, of clarity, of refinement, and of precision we pass by unheeding; we can see nothing there but coldness and uniformity; and we go back with eagerness to the fling and bravado that we love so well. It is as if we had become so accustomed to looking at boxers, wrestlers, and gladiators that the sight of an exquisite minuet produced no effect on us; the ordered dance strikes us as a monotony, for we are blind to the subtle delicacies of the dancers, which are fraught with such significance to the practised eye. (*BC*, 13–14)

Apart from this defense of the refined style, Strachey bases his case for Racine upon his strength as a psychologist, a dramatist engaged with the "mystery of the mind of man." "It is, perhaps, as a psychologist that Racine has achieved his most remarkable triumphs" (*BC*, 21).

Strachey proceeds by linking ideas already presented; clarity of language and psychological interest he connects to the expression of passion. Passion, of course, Strachey thought the most important element in life.[5] "But, as a rule, Racine's characters speak out most clearly when they are most moved, so that their words, at the height of passion, have an intensity of directness unknown in actual life" (*BC*, 24–25). Strachey's case for Racine is convincing. The essay is certainly one of his best critical pieces. He ends by referring to Racine alive on the contemporary stage: "To hear the words of Phèdre spoken by the mouth of Bernhardt. . . —that indeed is to come close to immortality, to plunge shuddering through infinite abysses, and to look, if only for a moment, upon eternal light" (*BC*, 28–29). It is interesting to note, here, the religious language of Strachey's response to art which, like religion, he had been inclined to see as a bag of tricks or, at best, as expression or pure form. Strachey's defense of Racine is, perhaps, his most significant contribution to literary criticism, for he helped to extend Racine's English reputation at a time when such a defense was necessary.

Before considering Strachey's first book, *Landmarks in French Literature,* a final example of his early critical writing, his introduction to Henry Frowde's 1908 reissue of Elizabeth Inchbald's *A Simple Story* should be discussed. Here his biographical and critical interests come together in a way that shows how at their best they were related and reinforced each other. Strachey begins by stating that "The merits of *A Simple Story* are of a kind peculiarly calculated to escape the notice of a generation of readers brought up on the fiction of the nineteenth century."[6] He adds that nineteenth-century fiction had an Elizabethan breadth of outlook on life. "Compared with *A Simple Story*," Strachey notes, "even the narrow canvasses of Jane Austen seem spacious pictures of diversified life" (*CC,* 135). Despite this narrowness, Strachey argues that Elizabeth Inchbald "can bring into her pages the living pressure of a human passion, she can invest [it] . . . —with the sense of reality itself—the pains, the triumphs, and the agitations of the human heart" (*CC,* 138). Strachey notes an autobiographical element in *A Simple Story* and writes: "One finds oneself speculating over the author, wondering what was her history, and how much of it was Miss Milner's" (*CC,* 139). Strachey's biography of his subject flows more naturally than usual from this speculation. He makes clear, indeed, the eventual connection between Elizabeth Inchbald's life and her art. Her "sense of reality" emerges from the courage with which she faced a difficult life.

In Strachey's hands, an interest in *A Simple Story* begets a straightforward account of Elizabeth Inchbald's life. Although Strachey has been criticized for affectation, he cherished simplicity. He preferred clarity of style and never sought to hide his meaning. He loved simplicity in eighteenth-century art and in the poetry of Wordsworth. In discussing Elizabeth Inchbald's novel, he achieves one of his best pieces of writing in which his interests in biography and literary criticism are fused. It was about two years after publishing this introductory essay that Strachey was invited at the age of thirty to write his first book. He was able to put the drudgery of reviewing behind him.

By the time H. A. L. Fisher asked Strachey to write *Landmarks in French Literature* in September 1910, Strachey had had considerable experience as an essayist and reviewer. But, apart from his dissertation on Warren Hastings which had failed to find a publisher, and his work on "English Letter Writers," he had no experience of undertaking a full-length study. However, he had written a number of essays and reviews on French topics, though as noted, far fewer than on English topics. In fact, Strachey was not especially strong in French. Though his mother was enthusiastic about French culture, and though Strachey himself received instruction in French from an early age, he did not speak the language with any confidence. He could read French acceptably, he visited France many times during his life, but he wrote French in his letters only as a secret language of love.

It will be useful to review briefly Strachey's involvement with French literature prior to writing *Landmarks in French Literature*. As early as

1903, in the *Independent Review*, Strachey published a highly critical review of Elizabeth Lee's translations of La Bruyère and Vauvenargues. Strachey's lifelong admiration for aphoristic wit is evident here. Two years later he published an article entitled "The Tragedies of Voltaire," again in the *Independent Review*. Though Voltaire was Strachey's hero, and though he wrote four or five articles about Voltaire and thought of writing a book about him, he was not impressed by Voltaire's tragedies. An article on Molière followed in the *Spectator* for 26 October 1907 in which Strachey argues persuasively against Saintsbury's view of Molière as simply the "master of the laugh."

On 21 December 1907 Strachey published a good review article of John Bailey's *The Claims of French Poetry* and of an anthology of French poetry by St. John Lucas. It is here that Strachey argued that "Racine, more than any other French poet, stands in need of an English interpreter."[7] Within six months Strachey had begun to supply the need himself with his essay "The Poetry of Racine" in the *New Quarterly* (June 1908). Merle describes this piece as one of Strachey's most admired critical productions. He notes further that Racine was the French author whom Strachey loved without reservation,[8] and that, although the article did not have a tremendous impact in 1908, it was placed at the head of Strachey's *Books and Characters* (1922), once Strachey had made a number of stylistic corrections to it. Strachey praises Racine's powers of concentration and selection, his sense of reality and ability to handle a vocabulary limited by the conventions of French dramatic practice.

In addition to the work already discussed, Strachey, by the time he received Fisher's commission to write *Landmarks in French Literature* for the Home University Library series, had also written on Malherbe, Corneille, La Rochefoucauld, Boileau, La Fontaine, Versailles, *le Siècle de Louis XIV*, Montesquieu, Rousseau, Hugo, and Verlaine. What is striking, though, is that almost all these authors and subjects fall in the period from 1660 to 1789, *le grand siècle*. Perhaps this is why his emphasis in *Landmarks* falls so heavily on the eighteenth-century period.

Strachey was comparatively unknown when he received the commission from Fisher. However, it is probable that Fisher had read some of his articles and so was not really taking a risk when he offered Strachey the commission. Strachey was given Mackail's *Latin Literature* in the same series to use as a model, and he read and reread Sainte-Beuve during the writing of *Landmarks*. Professor Dowden's study of French literature is also cited in Strachey's bibliography. The work on *Landmarks* took him a year, from September 1910 to September 1911.

Landmarks in French Literature is, given its dimensions, a précis of literary history. It runs from the *Chanson de Roland* to Verlaine, but it favors the epochs that Strachey knew best and preferred. Thus, the sense of balance for which Strachey's study is frequently praised is somewhat illusory. The book contains a large amount of material that Strachey had already used.

Strachey presents French literature as a conflict between the romantic and the classical spirit. He seeks to understand rather than judge French literature. The lack of close analysis in *Landmarks* can be attributed to the constraints of space, but Strachey rarely analyzes literature closely. In *Landmarks* he makes frequent use of culinary and seasonal metaphors: Villon's late medieval world is a world of winter, whereas the Renaissance is depicted as a world of spring.

Important authors are missing from Strachey's study, even from the period he favors: Madame de Lafayette, Mademoiselle de Scudèry, Madame de Sévigné, l'Abbé Prevost, Laclos, and Le Sage, for examples. More glaring, though, is the absence of important authors from the nineteenth century, the period hardest hit by Strachey's omissions: Merimeé, Nerval, Rimbaud, Mallarmé, and Zola. Indeed, Strachey may not have read Merimée, Nerval, or Mallarmé as he never refers to them in his correspondence.

Landmarks in French Literature (1912)

Landmarks in French Literature was published on 12 January 1912 and received a favorable notice in the *Times Literary Supplement*. The book's most signal deficiency, beyond those already noted, is Strachey's failure to give sufficient critical attention to Victor Hugo. Strachey had expressed negative views of *Hernani* in a letter to his mother of 5 August 1910. Despite the clear, stirring style of the book, Strachey uses questions, exclamations, exaggerations, and platitudes excessively. Some of his rhetorical effects are inaccurate, as when Racine is compared to a calm river, Shakespeare to a mountain torrent. Strachey then adds, "But still waters run deep."[9]

Nevertheless, most of the commentators such as Bower-Shore, Boas, Iyengar, Scott-James, Sanders, and Maurois praise this first book of Strachey's unreservedly. Desmond MacCarthy, however, spoke of it as "a little textbook of enthusiastical critical clichés." Strachey once expressed the view that "Perhaps the best test of a man's intelligence is his capacity for making a summary." This capacity is certainly present in *Landmarks in French Literature.*

That Strachey's literary critical method consists basically of either making a claim that he will attempt to substantiate or indicating a critical disagreement that he will attempt to resolve has already been noted. His normal procedure, thereafter, in essays and reviews is to provide a brief biography of his subject and offer illustrative quotations that are rarely analyzed in detail. He likes to generalize and to present aphoristic statements some of which can be perceptive but often lack authority because they are unsupported by analysis.

Far from deepening literary criticism like T. S. Eliot or F. R. Leavis, Strachey worked in an outworn form. He produced the kind of literary criticism that can be found, for example, in the Reverend Stopford Brooke's introduction to the *Golden Book of Coleridge.* Strachey is better remembered as a biographer than as a literary critic. *Landmarks in French Literature* is consistent with, rather than a significant development from, the methods of his earlier criticism. Its chief limitation is that it skates over the surface of French literature rather than plumbing its depths. Too frequently lacking supporting quotation, it is impressionistic at best.

In beginning his presentation of the development of French literature, Strachey appropriately considers the relationship of French literature to the French language. He also compares English literature to French literature; English literature he sees as bearing all the marks of a double origin, French literature he regards as homogenous. Strachey believes this quality is already visible in the earliest French works, the *chansons de geste* of which the *Chanson de Roland* is the most famous. However, rather than giving the reader an intimate feeling for the poetry of this famous work, he relies upon the externality of brief literary historical and generalized observation. Without analyzed quotation his comment on the poem's beauty of style has little meaning. He speaks of:

. . . eleventh-century France, with its aristocratic society, its barbaric vigour, its brutality, and its high sentiments of piety and honour. The beauty of the poem lies in the grand simplicity of its style.

. . . .

This great work—bleak, bare, gaunt, majestic—stands out, to the readers of to-day, like some huge mass of ancient granite on the far horizon of the literature of France. (*LFL,* 9–10)

Even in a short book this is surely not all that should be said about the *Chanson de Roland*.

Again, in contrasting the *chansons de geste* and the *Romans Bretons,* Strachey is content to rely on generalized contrast: "The spirit of these poems was very different from that of the *Chansons de Geste*. The latter were the typical offspring of the French genius—positive, definite, materialistic; the former were impregnated with all the dreaminess, the mystery, and the romantic spirituality of the Celt" (10). Strachey appears to be admitting the presence of the kind of duality that he denies to French literature at the outset of the study.

Strachey's ability to characterize a work briefly is often excellent, but he fails to supply the supporting quotation to clinch what seem like good points that he is making. Of *Aucassin et Nicolete* he says simply that its beauty is "at once fragile and imperishable" (13) and that its unknown author has succeeded in creating "a delicious atmosphere of delicate romance" (13).

The reader remains skeptical as Strachey hurries on into the thirteenth century and the beginnings of French prose. One doubts a critic who says of one of his subjects, in this case Jean de Meung, that he "was not a great artist; he wrote without distinction, and without sense of form; it is his bold and voluminous thought that gives him a high place in French literature" (19). How can an author who writes without distinction, and without sense of form show that he is a "bold and voluminous" thinker? Surely this is to separate form and content.

As with the discussion of *Aucassin et Nicolete,* when Strachey ends his far-too-brief survey of medieval French literature, his characterization of Villon sounds plausible, but once more lacks analyzed supporting quotation to make the observations convincing. Thus, Strachey writes of Villon:

The most self-communicative of poets, he has impressed his own personality on every line that he wrote. Into the stiff and complicated forms of the rondeau and rondel, the ballade and double ballade, with their limited rhymes and their enforced repetitions, he has succeeded in breathing not only the spirit of beauty, but the spirit of individuality. (23)

Perhaps this is true, but how is it done? Strachey fails to show his reader. He simply says that it is so.

The breathless pace continues into the second chapter. This chapter deals with the Renaissance. Strachey writes that "There is something dark and wintry about the atmosphere of the later Middle Ages" (26). This is critical impressionism at its most limited. The reader is not really learning about literature but is simply being moved along the road.

In writing of French Renaissance literature, Strachey notes the emancipation of the vernacular that was occurring throughout Europe at this time. He cites as an example du Bellay's *La défense et illustration de la langue Française.* Simultaneous with this development he remarks a renewed interest in the classics. The slackness of Strachey's writing is revealed when he writes that there were two results of classical imitation—yet he mentions only one. This is the show, but not the reality, of critical thought. "This desire to imitate classical literature led to two results. In the first place, it led to the invention of a great number of new poetical forms, and the abandonment of the old narrow and complicated conventions which had dominated the poetry of the Middle Ages" (30). Strachey never says what the second result was.

For Strachey it is not the *Pléiade,* but Rabelais who is the great exemplar of French Renaissance literature. The reader does not immediately dispute Strachey's judgment, nor necessarily his reading of literary history when he asserts "the spirit of the Renaissance—expansive, humourous, powerful, and, above all else, alive. Rabelais' book is the incarnation of the great reaction of his epoch against the gloom and the narrow asceticism of the Middle Ages" (35). However, as the study continues, one sees that this is a stage in Strachey's liberal-progressive interpretation of history, and that he has given no evidence of what he calls "the superstitious gloom and the narrow asceticism of the Middle Ages."

Chapter 3, the Age of Transition, prepares the way for the Age of Louis XIV, which, together with the eighteenth century, is what Strachey really wants to write about. Indeed, he opens his chapter: "From one point of view, indeed, this age may be considered the most important in the whole history of the literature, since it prepared the way for the most splendid and characteristic efflorescence in prose and poetry that France has ever known; without it, there would have been no *Grand Siècle*" (42). Here Strachey returns to comparison with English literature. Such comparisons are essential to literary history, but as with the need to analyze quotations, they need to be precise to be convincing. Strachey considers that literature is a profession in France and an amateur occupation in England, yet even in the period under discussion the cases of Ben Jonson and Shakespeare undermine the accuracy of the assertion.

Landmarks in French Literature, though it may note the authors and
works that the beginning student would need to read, hardly provides
the reader with a grounding in French literary history let alone con-
vinces him that certain works and authors are landmarks, or if they are,
why they are important. Thus, Strachey writes of the waves of
Corneille's verse and a weaving image (perhaps by association of sounds)
is used to describe it, yet without detailed demonstration little can be
made of this account of Corneille's poetry. "It is a strange kind of
poetry: not that of imaginative vision, of plastic beauty, of subtle
feeling; but that of intellectual excitement and spiritual strength" (52).

In the balance of the chapter Strachey credits Pascal in his *Lettres
Provinciales* with the creation of modern French prose, "the French prose
that we know to-day, the French prose which ranks by virtue of its
vigour, elegance and precision as a unique thing in the literature of the
world" (56). He comments that of "Earlier prose writers . . . none had
struck upon the really characteristically French note" (56). The reader
may ask what "the really characteristically French note" is, whether it is
something that Strachey could define if called upon to do so. Literary
criticism, it becomes clear, requires definition to be convincing.
Strachey says that the earlier writers of French prose "lacked form, and
those fine qualities of strength and clarity which form alone can give"
(56). But what is this mysterious "form"? Surely the reader should, at
least, be given some examples of it in operation if he is to gain an
inkling of what it is.

Pascal is credited with a simplicity that Strachey admires but does
not sufficiently emulate. His account of Pascal is one that Strachey
might with advantage have applied more fully to his own writings.
Considering the depth of Pascal's Christianity, Strachey's insistence
upon his modernism can be doubted. Surely there is more to Pascal's
medievalism than Strachey allows. There was, for example, a strong
tradition of Christian reason in the Middle Ages. Once more there is a
gulf between the claims Strachey makes and his capacity to supply
supporting evidence. Even if the reader would like to agree with
Strachey's judgment that "In sheer genius Pascal ranks among the very
greatest writers who have lived upon this earth. And his genius was not
simply artistic; it displayed itself no less in his character and (*sic*) in the
quality of his thought" (58), he is left wondering about the grounds for
Strachey's judgment.

The two longest chapters in the book concern the age of Louis XIV
and the eighteenth century, the periods of French literature that

Strachey knew best and about which he was the most enthusiastic. Naturally, one would expect him here to be at his best critically, yet the limitations of superficial treatment and unsupported argument remain. The balance of the book, in essence, sings the praises of Racine, Molière, and Voltaire. Strachey sees France at this point in her history as dominating the civilized world "through her literature and her manners" (62). He romanticizes Versailles: "When the morning sun was up and the horn was sounding down the long avenues, who would not wish, if only in fancy, to join the glittering cavalcade where the young Louis led the hunt in the days of his opening glory?"(64). This is the point to which the whole book has been moving: "When Louis XIV assumed the reins of government, France suddenly and wonderfully came to her maturity; it was as if the whole nation had burst into splendid flower" (62). This is the pivot, the center of *Landmarks in French Literature*.

Strachey presents Molière as occupying the same place in French literature as Cervantes in Spanish, Dante in Italian, or Shakespeare in English literature. Molière does not need to be defended critically as Racine does since outside France everyone accepts Molière as representing his country's highest achievement in literature. Nevertheless, Strachey says that Molière is the least classical of the great French classics. Strachey sees Molière as connected with the common earth and with humanity.

Molière's achievement is defined by Strachey thus: "Molière did for the comic element in French literature what Corneille had done for the tragic: he raised it to the level of serious art" (81). Strachey's account of Molière, though as usual it lacks the detailed analysis necessary to make it fully convincing, is one of the best discussions in the book in that Strachey perceives that Molière's genius reached beyond enslavement to the classical rules of art that dominated French culture in his time. Molière, Strachey persuades the reader, possessed the individuality and originality of the truly great artist.

As Strachey had noted in his earlier work on Racine, "Englishmen have always loved Molière. It is hardly an exaggeration to say that they have always detested Racine" (89). If "comprehension" was the key to Elizabethan tragedy, Strachey suggests that "concentration" is the important term in the case of Racine. Strachey's defense of Racine is essentially the same as it had been in his essay "The Poetry of Racine" (June 1908). But having claimed a Shakespearean prominence for Molière, it becomes difficult to make the same claim for Racine, so

Strachey tempers his claim somewhat. However, of *Phèdre* he states, "The play contains one of the most finished and beautiful, and at the same time one of the most overwhelming studies of passion in the literature of the world" (108). In spite of this, Strachey expresses the same bafflement in the face of Racine's religion as he did when confronted by Pascal's. He notes that at forty Racine quit the stage and entered a religious retreat. He adds, "One is tempted to see in his mysterious mortification an instance of that strain of disillusionment which runs like a dark thread through the brilliant texture of the literature of the *grand siècle*" (110). A confirmed modernist, in favor of enlightenment and progress, Strachey fails to understand Racine's and Pascal's rejection of the modern world.

It is to Voltaire that Strachey is most deeply drawn, in part because of Voltaire's mockery of religion. It is curious, though, that Voltaire like Madame du Deffand appears in Strachey's characterization as a kind of grinning skeleton. The reader sees Strachey as a puppet master of his prose creations. Thus, he writes of Voltaire:

His character was composed of a strange amalgam of all the most contradictory elements in human nature, and it would be difficult to name a single virtue or a single vice which he did not possess. (169)

It is difficult to grasp what Strachey is trying to do here. It is hard to believe in such a contradictory character or characterization. Presumably, Strachey is trying to represent the diversity of Voltaire, yet the contradiction presented arouses the suspicion that Strachey's own feelings of division are finding their way into the picture. Strachey's identification with Voltaire stems from his own cynicism and his rationalist view that life is entirely material, even though ultimately one finds suppressed religious elements in Strachey's nature rebelling against this narrow view.

When *Landmarks in French Literature* was published in January 1912 it was the culmination of his work as a literary critic. His biographical work had begun in essays and reviews but was not to find its full expression until *Eminent Victorians* six years later.

In his study of French literature Strachey concluded that while France had not produced a genius equal to Shakespeare, it was only England that had produced as many writers of the first rank as France. And even ancient Greece had not produced a Shakespeare. This should go some way toward dispelling the suspicion that Strachey was an inveterate anti-English Francophile.

In trying to assess the nature of the achievement of French literature, Strachey argues that beyond its devotion to truth, love of rhetoric, clarity, and generalizing power lies its "conscious search for ordered beauty; an unwavering, an indomitable pursuit of the endless glories of art" (247). Interestingly, it was precisely a principle of deliberation, of intention, of a "conscious search for ordered beauty" that Strachey was seeking in his own writing. With his early reviewing days behind him he was able to pursue this goal into the longer essays that led him up to and included *Eminent Victorians* (1918).

Chapter Three

The Critical Biographer:
Eminent Victorians (1918)

Overview

Between the publication of *Landmarks in French Literature* (1912) and
the appearance of *Eminent Victorians* (1918) Lytton Strachey changed
slowly from critic to biographer. In fact, this change was under way
even before the publication of *Landmarks in French Literature*. Indeed,
literary criticism was an alternative career that Strachey took up for a
time for the *Spectator* and other periodicals. His academic training had
been in history. Strachey did work on Warren Hastings as an undergraduate at Cambridge and also spent time on a postgraduate thesis on
the same subject. Besides, a fair number of Strachey's early essays and
reviews were biographical.

Gabriel Merle has noted that Strachey published nine biographical
essays and reviews on English topics between 1904 and 1909 and six on
French topics between 1906 and 1917. Significantly, the long essay
"Madame du Deffand," which appeared in the *Edinburgh Review* in
January 1913 and was collected in *Books and Characters* (1922) (a volume whose title suggests the changing emphasis in Strachey's career),
was the first occasion on which Strachey signed himself "Lytton
Strachey."[1] It should be noted, too, that in the period immediately
before the publication of *Landmarks in French Literature,* and shortly
afterwards, Strachey was struggling to find the right direction for
himself as a writer. Indeed, between 1908 and 1913 he made several
attempts to write fiction and drama as well as continuing to write
poetry.[2] Four chapters for a sketch of a novel called "Lord Pettigrew"
were completed between 1908 and 1911, while the short novel or
"joke" *Ermyntrude and Esmeralda* was completed in 1913. In drama,
Strachey struggled with "Essex: A Tragedy" in 1909 and completed "A
Son of Heaven," a tragic melodrama, in 1912. Interestingly, in "Essex:
A Tragedy" he concentrates upon the period from Essex's return from

Ireland to his arrest; he was to draw upon the same period later for *Elizabeth and Essex: A Tragical History* (1929).

Strachey at thirty-eight, at the time of the publication of *Eminent Victorians*, was essentially a critic, and primarily a literary critic who used an intuitive rather than meticulous method of analysis. Strachey's shift from criticism to biography was part of his attempt to separate art and life. In art he admired form, style, and even classic detachment, yet he was a romantic who wished to be able to break rules, an aesthete who cherished art for art's sake. Voltaire was the balanced stylist and ironist admired by Strachey's mother, and it was upon his style that Strachey sought to model his own. His adolescent admiration of Racine was followed by an admiration for Dostoyevski who forced Strachey to confront the human and the irrational. But the act of judging in literary criticism, which Strachey increasingly resisted, muffled his own creativity. This forced him to find another outlet for writing. He turned to man himself, imperceptibly switching his attention from criticism to biography. He found it easier to judge people than the works of art they produced.[3]

Strachey was deeply affected by the 1914–18 war. Through the influence of his brother James, Lytton became more involved in human affairs during this period, in particular with pacifism. His brother's articles on Freud for the *Spectator* (1910–12) and his "According to Freud" may also have stimulated Lytton's interest in the human psychology that became an important part of his biographical method.

Eminent Victorians is the first full fruit of Strachey's interest in a new kind of short biography that, despite its brevity, was deepened by new psychological interests. Through the use of psychology Strachey sought to uncover the subconscious motives for the actions of four important Victorians.

With the partial exception of General Gordon, all four of Strachey's subjects in *Eminent Victorians* (Cardinal Manning, Florence Nightingale, Dr. Thomas Arnold, and General Gordon) were extremely practical people of great energy who Strachey (an extremely impractical person himself) sought to discredit by attributing dubious or unworthy motivations to their activities. Manning's efforts to alleviate human suffering are seen to cloak a stronger desire for personal success; Florence Nightingale likewise is depicted as diverting or sublimating her sexual life into a life of intense practicality achieved through the sometimes cruel manipulation of others. Rather than the liberal Christian headmaster who reformed the English public school system, Dr. Arnold is seen as a crude zealot, while the Christian warrior General Charles George Gordon is reduced to a surreptitious brandy drinker and religious fanatic. The portraits are designed to diminish the reader's sense of the achievements of these eminent Victorians to futile lives of energetic bustle. Strachey sees the Victorian age as ultimately responsible for World War I. The book is an act of rebellion, a gesture of patricide.

While satirizing his Victorian subjects, Strachey sought to reform the art of biography. He wished to introduce brief, sharply written, ironic portraits. At a time when a new poetry was beginning in the work of Ezra Pound and T. S. Eliot, Strachey was attempting to create a new biography. His effort can be seen as part of a larger modern movement in arts and letters generally to, in Pound's words, "make it new." Strachey's liberal love of peace, tolerance, independence, and sexual freedom led him to attack the age into which he had been born and which he presumably felt had repressed him and from which he was struggling to free himself. The division and conflict in himself he grafts onto his subjects in *Eminent Victorians*. He sees each of them as beset with contradictions that, in his view, proceed from origins in sexual repression.

This is not the place to review the development of biography as a genre;[4] suffice it to say that the publication of *Eminent Victorians* in 1918 was an important step in the development of a genre that reaches back four thousand years. Essentially, Strachey did two things that in the long run have proved incompatible: he tried to write psychological biographies that were also brief. However, time has shown that if psychoanalytic work is to be done properly, both detail and space are required. It is ironic, therefore, that the two best and most complete studies of Strachey to date, Michael Holroyd's (1967) and Gabriel Merle's (1980), are both in two volumes.

Lytton Strachey's new approach to biography was not unprecedented and the anti-Victorianism he is sometimes credited with fathering was well under way within the Victorian period itself. Within biography, Froude's *Reminiscences* of Carlyle were not uncritical, nor was Purcell's two-volume life of Cardinal Manning from which Strachey drew for his own portrait. Ian Ker, reviewing the most recent biography of Cardinal Manning, points out that an argument between Manning and his successor as Archbishop of Westminster, Henry Vaughan, over the latter's attendance at a Licensed Victuallers' dinner when Manning was conducting a crusade against drink, led to Manning's changing his will to remove Vaughan as his literary executor. Vaughan was later to remark that this action cost Manning his posthumous reputation because his papers fell into the hands of the Catholic journalist E. S. Purcell who claimed he had been appointed Manning's official biographer. It was Purcell's sensational *Life of Manning* (1895) that inspired Strachey's "notorious profile . . . of an ambitious and unscrupulous ecclesiastic."[5]

Ker's designation of Strachey's characterization of Cardinal Manning as a "notorious profile" is exact. Indeed, *Eminent Victorians* was originally to have been called *Victorian Silhouettes*. But it was not just Froude and Purcell who pushed Strachey in the direction he was to take with biography. Virginia Woolf's father, Leslie Stephen, as editor of *The Dictionary of National Biography* had given biography a new brevity and scientific basis. Also, Edmund Gosse, whose *Father and Son* (1907), was an anti-Victorian critique, criticized the standard two-volume biography.[6] Finally, Sidney Lee's *Principles of Biography* (1911) argued against excess of detail because such excess failed to transmit personality. So, on 17 October 1912 Strachey wrote to Lady Ottoline Morrell, "I am . . . beginning a mere experiment in the way of a short condensed biography of Cardinal Manning—written from a slightly cynical standpoint."

Strachey's "Preface" to *Eminent Victorians* is no less controversial than the rest of the book. Its argument is curiously illogical, suggesting that the history of the Victorian age will never be written, not because we know too little about it but because we know too much. This becomes a license for Strachey to be selective. Hamlet-like he argues that by indirection he will find direction out, "It is not by the direct method of a scrupulous narration that the explorer of the past can hope to depict that singular epoch." Respecting truth, the reader is inclined to ask why not? But Strachey offers his own selective approach as "wisdom." "If he [the explorer of the past] is wise, he will adopt a subtler strategy. He will row out over the great ocean of material, and lower down into it, here and there, a little bucket, which will bring up to the light of day some characteristic specimen, from those far depths, to be examined with a careful curiosity."[7] His Victorian subjects, then, "an ecclesiastic, an educational authority, a woman of action, and a man of adventure" as he calls them, he sees as fish whom he wishes to examine. He had earlier characterized Amy Lowell's method of examining French symbolist poets, to whom she was unsympathetic, as like examining "submarine fishes."[8] While unsympathetic to Lowell's use of detached examination, Strachey, nevertheless, uses it himself.

Passing over Johnson, Boswell, Lockhart, and Carlyle to say nothing of Walton or Aubrey, Strachey writes: "The art of biography seems to have fallen on evil times in England. We have had, it is true, a few masterpieces, but we have never had, like the French, a great biographical tradition(10). He concludes with a justification of his brief method that is also highly problematic:

To preserve, for instance a becoming brevity—a brevity which excludes everything that is redundant and nothing that is significant—that, surely, is the first duty of the biographer. The second, no less surely, is to maintain his own freedom of spirit. It is not his business to be complimentary; it is his business to lay bare the facts of the case, as he understands them, dispassionately, impartially, and without ulterior intentions. (10)

It is Strachey's claim to impartiality and lack of "ulterior intentions" that is particularly surprising here especially in view of his manipulation of his sources.[9]

Cardinal Manning

Robert Gray, Cardinal Manning's most recent biographer, argues that Strachey's "short condensed biography" of the cardinal amounts to little more than a sticking together of snippets from Purcell's *Life* and says that no one could be less sympathetic to Manning than Strachey. Yet he wonders, finally, about Strachey's attitude to religion at the end of his life.[10] In essence, Strachey tries to depict Manning as a man who used religion to satisfy worldly ambition. But the portrait does not stop there, for it is an attack on religion itself. Both the Roman Catholic Church and the Church of England in its Oxford Movement phase are attacked. Strachey was writing his play "A Son of Heaven" at the same time as his portrait of Manning, and the portrait contains theatrical elements, not least in the dramatized conflict between Manning and John Henry Newman. Newman is presented as the dove destroyed by Manning as eagle; Manning suppresses Newman as he himself rises. In these characterizations Strachey distorts history to strengthen his case. For example, Newman's tears of nostalgia at Littlemore (near Oxford) are presented by Strachey as tears of grief at being denied an Oxford oratory through Manning's machinations.[11]

The difficulty with Strachey's partial portrait of Manning as a man governed solely by worldly ambition is that it is not sufficiently plausible. The reader asks, for example, what if Manning's wife had not died and he had been unable to become a Roman Catholic priest? Too much of Strachey's portrait depends on inference and innuendo. Can one believe that Pio Nono did strike a bargain with Manning on his early visit to Rome? The opening of the portrait shows what Strachey seeks to achieve in painting Manning: "Henry Edward Manning was born in 1807 and died in 1892. His life was extraordinary in many ways, but its interest for the modern inquirer depends mainly upon two considerations—the light which his career throws upon the spirit of his age, and the psychological problems suggested by his inner history" (p. 13). Strachey suggests that Manning's career provides an illustrative example of the spirit of his age. He then shows Manning as a hypocrite who uses religion as a mask. He reduces Manning's motivations to those of worldly ambition and so attacks the whole spirit of the Victorian age. The suggestion of "psychological problems" in this context therefore seems to be extended beyond Manning to the Victorians in general.

Manning's practicality is scorned and he is depicted as lacking both saintliness and learning. The reader is told disparagingly that had Manning lived in the Middle Ages he might have been an Innocent though never a Francis or an Aquinas. However, a satirist, who set some store by the values that Manning is supposed to lack, would appear more plausible than one whose cynicism has no time for them. At the end of the brief opening section of the portrait, Strachey asks a series of questions about Manning's rise to prominence that suggest that his success was due less to merit than to guile, and that it was a "soft place" (13) at the heart of the apparently "scientific and progressive" (13) society of nineteenth-century England that allowed Manning to succeed.

In terms of Manning's eventual career and success in that career, Strachey fails to see the bankruptcy of Manning's father as posing a problem for him. Strachey's cynical irony refers to the death of Manning's wife as "the merciful removal of his wife" (19). His use of the word "merciful" here is utterly ironic.

As an example of the cynical humor and irony of "Cardinal Manning" the following passage is representative. It shows that Strachey has no time for religion and little sympathy with those Victorians who suffered a loss of faith:

. . . James Anthony [Froude], together with Arthur Clough, the poet, went through an experience which was more distressing in those days than it has since become: they lost their faith. With this difference, however, that while in Froude's case the loss of faith turned out to be rather like the loss of a heavy portmanteau, which one afterwards discovers to have been full of old rags and brickbats, Clough was made so uneasy by the loss of his that he went looking for it everywhere as long as he lived; but somehow he never could find it. On the other hand, Keble and Pusey continued for the rest of their lives to dance in an exemplary manner upon the tight-rope of High Anglicanism; in such an exemplary manner, indeed, that the tight-rope has its dancers still. (41–42)

The curious thing, here, is that the humorous combination of the spiritual and material in the image of faith as a portmanteau is clearly Dickensian, yet Strachey claimed to be bored by Dickens. Strachey's attitude toward religion is skeptical throughout.

Irony and satire are revealed once more in the tone of the following sentence, which implies Manning's lack of intellectual independence: "At last, in the seclusion of his library, Manning turned in an agony to those old writings which had provided Newman with so much instruction and assistance; perhaps the Fathers would do something for him as well" (50). The colloquial flippancy of the last clause reveals Strachey's satiric intent.

Besides irony, Strachey uses innuendo. "In the light of after-events, one would be glad to know what precisely passed at that mysterious interview of his with the Pope, three years before his conversion" (56). Too, Strachey quotes comments that Talbot and Newman are supposed to have made without supplying any sources, a practice that undermines the reader's confidence in the authenticity of the quotations. All the reader is offered is a list of books at the end of each biographical portrait. A much greater show of scholarship is made in *Queen Victoria* where Strachey's approach is less stringently satirical—comic rather than ironic.

The jealous thwarting of Newman by Manning is exaggerated by Strachey to further disparage Manning's character. Manning is presented as rising at Newman's expense; his treatment of Newman is seen as a further facet of Manning's worldly ambition. Yet Strachey's own partiality continuously emerges from the irony that he finds irresistible: "the rights of democracies, the claims of science, the sanctity of free speech, the principles of toleration—were categorically denounced, and their supporters abandoned to the Divine wrath. Yet it was observed that the modern world proceeded as before" (82). It is clear that Strachey is for "the modern world" and against the Catholic Church.

Indeed, his portrait of Manning is like that of Robert Browning's Bishop in "The Bishop Orders His Tomb" in its emphasis on worldliness; the central recounting of the motivation of Manning's conversion with its shifty logic is representative of the portrait—indeed, of *Eminent Victorians* as a whole:

When Manning joined the Church of Rome he acted under the combined impulse of the two dominating forces in his nature. His preoccupation with the supernatural might, alone, have been satisfied within the fold of the Anglican communion; and so might his preoccupation with himself: the one might have found vent in the elaborations of High Church ritual, and the other in the activities of a bishopric. But the two together could not be quieted so easily. (55)

The intention of this passage and what follows it is to characterize Manning as a "superstitious egotist" (55). In the same paragraph Strachey uses animal images to reduce Manning's stature: like a dog he "scented nobler quarry" or like a horse he has "a bit between his teeth." Strachey's attitude to Manning's beliefs is further revealed in the phrase "illimitable pretensions" (55) which for a believer would read "illimitable powers." In *Eminent Victorians* Strachey's method is essentially the method of irony which is present throughout.

Florence Nightingale

Strachey's selective approach to the history of the Victorian age continues as he again brings "to the light of day some characteristic specimen" (9)—this time Florence Nightingale, the subject of the second portrait in *Eminent Victorians*. In the case of Manning, Strachey presents piety and good works cloaking worldly ambition; in Florence Nightingale the case is much the same, except that Strachey is more impressed by powerful women than he is by powerful men. Consequently, a more balanced and sympathetic portrait emerges. But still his intention is iconoclastic. He wants to shatter the legend of Longfellow's "Lady with a Lamp," though not necessarily shatter the lamp itself.

Two letters that Strachey wrote to his mother and his brother within a day of each other, while he was still working on his portrait of Cardinal Manning, make his attitude and approach to Nightingale clear. To his mother on 15 January 1914—after reading Sir Edward

Cook's life of Nightingale, which he cites with approval in his Preface to *Eminent Victorians* and which Merle argues influenced Strachey's approach to biography[12]—he indicates that he thinks Florence Nightingale "a capable woman but rather disagreeable in various ways—a complete egotist, also full of a very tiresome religiosity, and I don't think really intelligent." He thinks that she never possessed a scientific grasp of things despite spending her life in medical concerns. However, he realizes that she would not have been so effective if she had been less self-sufficient. He observes that if Nightingale had died in the Crimea, many reforms that she worked for later would not have been accomplished. Strachey's attitude to her is more ambivalent than his attitude toward Manning. He presents no redeeming virtues in Manning's case, but he sees some practical benefits issuing from the work of Florence Nightingale.

The following day his letter to his brother James is more direct: "I have just been reading the book I might have written. I'm glad I didn't, as I couldn't have satisfied anybody. She was a terrible woman—though powerful. And certainly a wonderful book might have been made out of her, from the cynical point of view. Of course the Victorian Age is fairly reeking all over it. What a crew they were!" Here Strachey seems to indicate that he might have been entrusted with the biography of Florence Nightingale that Sir Edward Cook, in fact, wrote. As he admits, it was probably a good thing that he did not undertake the task. But one does get an insight into how he worked in *Eminent Victorians;* he took a detailed biography of his subject—such as Purcell's of Manning, Cook's of Florence Nightingale, Stanley's of Dr. Arnold, and several of General Gordon—and stripped it down to fit his satiric purpose or "cynical point of view." In the letter to James one sees Strachey's lifelong fascination with powerful women (Florence Nightingale, Queen Victoria, Elizabeth I) but, more important, it reveals the desire to rewrite Cook's book and to attack the Victorian age.

The opening of the second portrait in *Eminent Victorians* shows the "cynical point of view" in action. The deflationary tone found here is typical of Strachey's tone throughout the book:

Every one knows the popular conception of Florence Nightingale. The saintly, self-sacrificing woman, the delicate woman of high degree who threw aside the pleasures of a life of ease to succour the afflicted, the Lady with the Lamp, gliding through the horrors of the hospital at Scutari, and consecrating with the radiance of her goodness the dying soldier's couch—the vision is familiar to all. But the truth was different. The Miss Nightingale of fact was not as facile fancy painted her. She worked in another fashion, and towards another end; she moved under the stress of an impetus which finds no place in popular imagination. A Demon possessed her. Now demons, whatever else they may be, are full of interest. And so it happens that in the real Miss Nightingale there was more that was interesting than in the legendary one; there was also less that was agreeable. (111)

Strachey is the shrewd, unmasking biographer—the psychoanalyst who can flush out the true, though hidden, motive. "A Demon possessed her." A short, revelatory sentence is used to unmask the truth (as Strachey sees it) about Florence Nightingale. But the truth must be made to appear as exciting as the legend, so the reader is told, "Now demons, whatever else they may be, are full of interest. And it so happens that in the real Miss Nightingale there was more that was interesting than in the legendary one; there was also less that was agreeable."

What, then, does Strachey have to reveal about Florence Nightingale? As with Manning, the reader is given a portrait of zealous earnestness that leaves a trail of destruction in its wake, with the difference that Strachey respects Nightingale's creation of the nursing profession whereas Manning's philanthropic works leave him cold. Like Manning to Newman, Florence Nightingale is an eagle or tiger to Sidney Herbert's stricken hind. Where Manning builds his own career and thwarts Newman, Nightingale is seen to make use of and finally exhaust Sidney Herbert with her reforming enterprises.

However, there are elements in Nightingale's character and story that resist Strachey's satire. Her rejection of the comforts of upper-middle-class life for a life of service is hard to satirize as is her rejection of Victorian marriage. Though Strachey presents her "demon" as "that singular craving of hers to be *doing* something" (112), he is forced to admit that Nightingale is responsible for replacing Mrs. Gamp with the modern nurse. Struggle as he will to avoid complimentary language, he notes that, "Certainly, things have changed since those days; and that they *have* changed is due, far more than to any other human being, to Miss Nightingale herself" (113). Indeed, the worst that Strachey can charge Nightingale with is being a "workaholic" (in our terms) who drove others as well as herself, who suppressed her sexual energies or diverted them into her obsession with organization, "The most powerful and the profoundest of all the instincts of humanity laid claim upon her. But it rose before her, that instinct, arrayed—how could it be otherwise?—in the inevitable habiliments of a Victorian marriage; and she had the strength to stamp it underfoot" (114).

As Strachey's respect for Nightingale grows, his satire begins to be directed against government bureaucratic inefficiency and bungling, especially in the Crimea. His attack recalls that of Dickens's *Little Dorrit* (1856), which was, of course, contemporary with the Crimean War. Strachey, perhaps echoing Dickens, writes, "the evil was in reality that worst of all evils—one which has been caused by nothing in particular and for which no one in particular is to blame" (117).

An interesting item, which Strachey cannot resist mentioning, is that "Among the numerous letters which she [Florence Nightingale] received on her departure [for the Crimea] was one from Dr. Manning, who at that time was working in comparative obscurity as a Catholic priest in Bayswater" (116–17). Although this detail does nothing to advance Strachey's case against Manning, it provides a link between these "eminent Victorians."

The picture that emerges of Florence Nightingale overcoming administrative incompetence in the Crimea is entirely sympathetic, even moving. Strachey's narrative style becomes varied and flexible as he responds to Florence Nightingale's virtues:

Her good will could not be denied, and her capacity could not be disregarded. With consummate tact, with all the gentleness of supreme strength, she managed at last to impose her personality upon the susceptible, overwrought, discouraged, and helpless group of men in authority who surrounded her. She stood firm; she was a rock in an angry ocean; with her alone was safety, comfort, life. . . . order came upon the scene, and common sense, and forethought, and decision. (122)

Nightingale disarms the confused Crimean administrators and, temporarily at least, her biographer as well. It is hard to reduce her to the subject of a cheap debunking exercise. Strachey, at least, makes that concession. In fact, the serious and convincing point that he has to make in the portrait is that Florence Nightingale's triumph was, in truth, a triumph of organization. He records that it took her six months of labor until May 1855 to be able to "look with something like satisfaction at the condition of the Scutari hospitals" (129) by which time the mortality rate had fallen from forty-two per hundred to twenty-two per thousand. She received the praise of Queen Victoria as "one who has set so bright an example to our sex" (132).

Strachey goes on to discuss the fact that Florence Nightingale lived for fifty years after the Crimean War, and, indeed, "her real life began at the very moment when, in the popular imagination, it had ended" (133). Queen Victoria, he says, was reported to have said of her "Such a *head!* I wish we had her at the War Office" (135).

Because she was a woman, Florence Nightingale was forced to capitalize heavily on the advantages she had, such as her social position and connections. She worked through Sidney Herbert to whom she had already poured out her soul during her Crimean days. As Strachey puts it, "it was through the man that the woman must work her will" (139). For Strachey, whose mother had wanted him to be either viceroy of India or poet laureate, this fulfillment of a woman's will through a man was familiar. It makes him sympathetic to Sidney Herbert, who he sees as pressed to death by Florence Nightingale's demands: "the tigress has her claws in the quivering haunches; and then . . . he who set out to be of use to Miss Nightingale was apt to find, before he had gone very far, that he was in truth being made use of in good earnest—to the very limit of his endurance and his capacity" (139–140).

The reductive animal images that the reader has seen at work already in the characterization of Manning as an eagle and Newman as a dove are continued into the Florence Nightingale portrait. So when Strachey comes to present her investigations into health in the army following the Crimean War, her political opponent Lord Panmure is called the Bison: " 'the Bison was bullyable'—the hide was the hide of a Mexican buffalo, but the spirit was the spirit of an Alderney calf" (142). Indeed, although the animal images are generally reductive, Strachey's satire is directed for the most part against Nightingale's opponents. For his attitude to Florence Nightingale was ambivalent; he found her a "terrible woman" but was, even so, in awe of her power. Her achievements he admits; her *Notes affecting the Health, Efficiency, and Hospital Administration of the British Army,* he writes, "remains to this day [1918] the leading authority on the medical administration of armies" (143).

Yet, to catch the full force of Strachey's ambivalent attitude toward his subject, one should note that he sees Florence Nightingale's preoccupation, or in his terms obsession, with health as itself a kind of sickness: "she carried that with her which made health impossible. Her desire for work could now scarcely be distinguished from mania . . . Her wits began to turn, and there was no holding her. She worked like

a slave in a mine. . . . (144). Meanwhile, still ravenous for more and
yet more work, her activities had branched out into new directions.
The Army in India claimed her attention" (147).

Nevertheless, Florence Nightingale continues to prove resistant to
Strachey's satire. He sees her triumphing over illness, though the triumph itself is, in his view, another form of illness. So, when Sidney
Herbert dies, Strachey struggles to avoid holding Nightingale responsible, though that surely is his implication: "When the onward rush of a
powerful spirit sweeps a weaker one to its destruction, the common-
places of the moral judgement are better left unmade" (149).

Thus, the division in Strachey, already noted, is inevitably present in
his characterization of Florence Nightingale; his ambiguous portrait of
a character of weakness and strength is in many respects a portrait of
himself, "an invalid who was too weak to walk downstairs and who
worked harder than most Cabinet Ministers. . . . Lying on her sofa in
the little upper room in South Street, she combined the intense vitality
of a dominating woman of the world with the mysterious and romantic
quality of a myth" (152). Strachey seems to admit finally that there are
grounds for the popular legend, though he has tried to present a more
complex analysis of Florence Nightingale. However, his skeptical desire to attack and reduce triumphs in the end. It makes his portrait of
Florence Nightingale consistent with the other three portraits, though
it is the most sympathetic in *Eminent Victorians*.

Dr. Arnold

Strachey's portrait of Dr. Thomas Arnold is the briefest, most bi-
ased, and perfunctory in *Eminent Victorians*. He finished his portrait of
Florence Nightingale on 23 June 1915 and did nothing further on
Eminent Victorians for six months.[13] To his mother he wrote on 12
December 1915, "I am (also) engaged in a short life of Dr. Arnold (of
Rugby), which is a distinctly lugubrious business, though my hope is
to produce something out of it which may be entertaining. He was a
self-righteous blockhead, but unlike most of his kind, with enough
energy and determination in him to do a good deal of damage, as our
blessed Public Schools bear witness."[14] Though his wish was to amuse,
one can see that from the beginning Strachey set out to characterize Dr.
Arnold as a "self-righteous blockhead." Although the portrait is only
ten thousand words long, it took Strachey ten months to write where
the Florence Nightingale portrait had taken him only five.

During the winter of 1915–16 Strachey was preoccupied with the conscription issue and that summer with Dora Carrington. He was already beginning to think about writing a biography of Queen Victoria. The difference between "Dr. Arnold" and Strachey's other three subjects is that they all sacrificed inner and domestic harmony for ambition, at least in Strachey's characterization of them, whereas Dr. Arnold was a married man with ten children. The portrait of Arnold is presented in four unnumbered divisions and is characterized by uninterrupted irony.[15] Strachey laughs at the supposed shortness of Arnold's legs, attacks his repressive character, but his religion is Strachey's favorite target. The short legs, according to Aldous Huxley, were entirely Strachey's own invention.[16]

George K. Simson in his important work on Strachey's handling of his sources for *Eminent Victorians* points out how thoroughly Strachey distorts, for his satiric purpose, what he had read in Stanley's life of Dr. Arnold.[17] He notes excisions within quotations from letters, that Dr. Arnold was of middle height rather than having short legs. He points out that Strachey changes a certain stiffness that Stanley notes in Arnold's behavior before he went to university into a lifelong pomposity. He calls attention to Strachey's strategic use of quotation marks to suggest more sources than he actually used. An old pupil of Arnold's to whom Strachey alludes is, in fact, Stanley. Yet, the many good things that Stanley has to say of his old headmaster are omitted. Arnold's own doubts about his success are suppressed. His feeling that he is doing as much as is humanly possible about modern language learning is made to appear as limited insularity.

In his portrait of Arnold, Strachey gives the impression that Arnold's reading was limited to the writers of Greek tragedy, Propertius and Aristophanes, whereas Stanley indicates that Arnold had also read Homer, Virgil, Shakespeare, Dante, and Goethe. Also, Strachey tries to make Arnold appear condescending about music whereas Arnold, in fact, suffered from tone deafness. In his suffering he is reported to have said of flowers, "they are my music." Arnold's comment on Wordsworth's lines in "Ode: Intimations of Immortality. . ." about the "meanest flower" that there was "something in them of a morbid feeling" is reduced in Strachey's hands to "He found the sentiment morbid." Arnold is made to appear anti-French in his comment on the French not eating fish with a knife, but Simson notes that Strachey does not supply the full context of Arnold's remark. The extent of the distortion is revealed in Strachey's way of handling the following quotation from Dr. Arnold's journal: "And then the thought of my own private life, so full of comforts, is very startling, when I contrast it with the lot of millions, whose portion is so full of distress or of trouble." Strachey stops the quotation after the word "startling" and then adds "He was puzzled." This is a piece of complete misrepresentation. Simson calls it, "one of the cruellest cheats of the book." Arthur Hugh Clough, Dr. Arnold's best student, is also, of course, misrepresented throughout *Eminent Victorians*.

Strachey takes W. G. Ward's part over Arnold's in their debates. He stretches a day that Arnold spent in bed after an exhausting debate with Ward out to a risible "thirty-six hours." Strachey's portrait of Dr. Arnold is one-dimensional, and this considerably disrupts the artistic integrity of *Eminent Victorians* as a whole, so different is its tone and method of presentation.[18]

None of the exploratory ambiguity or subtlety of the portrait of Florence Nightingale is evident in Strachey's depiction of Dr. Arnold. The portrait is, in fact, a piece of flat caricature. Strachey picks up Stanley's reference to an early "stiffness and formality" in his pre-university letters to pillory Arnold:

It is true that, as a schoolboy, a certain pompousness in the style of his letters home suggested to the more clear-sighted among his relatives the possibility that young Thomas might grow up into a prig; but, after all, what else could be expected from a child, who, at the age of three, had been presented by his father, as a reward for proficiency in his studies, with the twenty-four volumes of Smollett's *History of England*? (163)

Of course, J. S. Mill was learning Greek at the age of three and Strachey himself was writing poetry at a remarkably early age, yet this, perhaps, is just the point. Strachey it seems, is protesting against the Victorians' overearnest application to learning in early childhood. Arnold, in Strachey's hands here, is portrayed as a victim of a system that Strachey finds repressive.

Nevertheless, the reductive nature of Strachey's satire is seen early in the portrait. He uses the same technique that links heavy portmanteaus and loss of faith in the presentation of Froude and Clough in the Manning portrait. Strachey creates reductive irony by linking unrelated subjects taken from quite different orders of experience. Thus, Dr. Arnold's aversion to early rising is inappropriately related to his doubts about the Trinity. "This weakness too he overcame, yet not quite so successfully as his doubts upon the doctrine of the Trinity" (164). Strachey follows this by implying that Arnold's seriousness was in reality a failure of intelligence, "And yet—why was it? Was it in the lines of the mouth or the frown on the forehead?—it was hard to say, but it was unmistakable—there was a slightly puzzled look upon the face of Dr. Arnold" (165).

Strachey abominates what Arnold holds dear. This is the reason for the caricature. Where Arnold values morality above intellect, Strachey sees things the other way. Strachey indicates that in responding to the Reverend Bowdler's view of the Public Schools as "nurseries of vice" (166), Arnold places moral above intellectual reform. Arnold's priorities stand revealed as, of course, do Strachey's. Arnold sought to make the English Public Schools places of Christian education. In his view, "what we must look for here is, first, religious and moral principle; secondly, gentlemanly conduct; thirdly, intellectual ability" (167). Though anathema to Strachey, this was sufficient to Squire Brown (of *Tom Brown's Schooldays*): " 'What is he sent to school for?. . .If he'll only turn out a brave, helpful, truth-telling Englishman, and a Christian, that's all I want.' " Strachey comments critically, "That was all; and it was that that Dr Arnold set himself to accomplish" (167).

In part, it is Strachey's own unhappiness at Abbotsholme and Leamington College, and, perhaps, his brother James's experience at Rugby that lead to his irony about Arnold's work there. So of the Praepostor or prefect system, of the Sixth-Form-governed school he writes, "He would treat the boys at Rugby as Jehovah had treated the Chosen People: he would found a theocracy; and there would be Judges in Israel. . . .The boys were to work out their own salvation, like the human race. He himself, involved in awful grandeur, ruled remotely, through his chosen instruments, from an inaccessible heaven" (168). Like Manning and Florence Nightingale, Arnold is seen by Strachey as an egotist who wishes to cast himself in a divine role. In fact, Arnold made friends of his senior students, which is surely the reason for the admiration that men like Clough, Stanley, and his son Matthew felt for him. Strachey, however, wishes to disparage Arnold's achievements.

Though Strachey complains that "in the school chapel the centre of Dr Arnold's system of education was inevitably fixed," he is forced to admit that "he read the Psalms with such conviction that boys would often declare, after hearing him, that they understood them now for the first time" (172). Of Arnold's relationship to the local community, Strachey writes, "Dr. Arnold himself occasionally visited them, in

Rugby; and the condescension with which he shook hands with old men and women of the working classes was long remembered in the neighborhood" (175). But does Dr. Arnold's action here necessarily bear the patronizing construction that Strachey puts on it? There must have been many Victorian headmasters who would never have dreamed of shaking hands with local people at all.

Every aspect of Arnold's endeavor is attacked by Strachey. Arnold's work as a historian is dismissed. Strachey is contemptuous of Arnold's idea of history, while his admiration for Gibbon's is unbounded. Even Arnold the family man becomes the object of Strachey's ridicule. Ostensibly, Strachey is discussing the seventeen volumes of work that Arnold left at his death, but he makes the discussion serve another purpose—to ridicule the family man: "It was no wonder that Carlyle, after a visit to Rugby, should have characterized Dr Arnold as a man of 'unhasting, unresting diligence.' Mrs. Arnold, too, no doubt agreed with Carlyle. During the first eight years of their married life, she bore him six children; and four more were to follow" (179). It hardly seems fair to attack Dr. Arnold for the number of children he had, especially when Strachey's parents had as many themselves.

Dr. Arnold's pride in his country is ridiculed as jingoism: " 'a thorough English gentleman—Christian, manly, and enlightened—is more, I believe, than Guizot or Sismondi could comprehend; it is a finer specimen of human nature than any other country, I believe, could furnish.' " (181). Finally, Dr. Arnold's best student, Arthur Clough, is used against him. Strachey caricatures Clough as a youth with weak ankles and a solemn face, preoccupied with moral problems, who, despite his education at Arnold's Rugby, was wracked by doubts at Oxford. Strachey depicts Clough as spending the remainder of his life lamenting his lost faith in prose and verse, and "doing up brown paper parcels for Florence Nightingale" (183).

The portrait of Clough (for whose difficulties Strachey appears to hold Dr. Arnold responsible) is as partial as the portrait of Dr. Arnold himself. Clough's "weak ankles" are presumably meant to parallel Dr. Arnold's short legs, but Clough was a strong swimmer and an accomplished soccer goalkeeper whose weak ankles are as much a Stracheyan fiction as Dr. Arnold's short legs. Strachey's antipathy throughout *Eminent Victorians* to the author of *Amours de Voyage, Dipsychus,* and "The Latest Decalogue" is hard to understand, for Clough was as keen a critic of Victorian conventions as Strachey himself.

Strachey's indictment of Arnold is of a man who he believes changed the face rather than the inner life of English education: "he threw the whole weight of his influence into the opposite scale, and the ancient system became more firmly established than ever" (187). It is clear that Strachey's intention is to disparage Arnold's achievements as much as possible. However, his narrow intention is itself a limitation and the caricature he presents of Dr. Arnold makes it the least effective portrait in *Eminent Victorians*.

The End of General Gordon

The final portrait in *Eminent Victorians* depicts General Gordon. Like Strachey's portrait of Florence Nightingale, this portrait fluctuates between satire and sympathy. Though Strachey seeks to reduce Gordon to a brandy-drinking religious fanatic, he cannot help but admire Gordon's individuality and courage. This leads him to produce a portrait as complex as that of Florence Nightingale. Strachey finds that, in spite of himself, he is impressed by both Florence Nightingale and General Gordon, so that D. H. Lawrence's maxim "Trust the tale and not the teller" has to be borne in mind in both cases.

It is not without significance that the title of the final portrait is "The End of General Gordon." What interests Strachey particularly, as in many of his portraits, is the death of his hero or heroine. Strachey began his portrait of General Gordon even before he had finished that of Dr. Arnold. He had read Lord Cromer's *Modern Egypt* (1907) and in 1912 J. O. P. Bland on China and Li Hung Chang. With the help of these two works Strachey could present either end of General Gordon's career.[19] He began to speak of doing his Gordon portrait in 1914. Its thirty thousand words were completed within a year.

General Gordon was sent to the Sudan on 18 January 1884 at the urging of Lord Hartington and the Imperial faction in Gladstone's Liberal cabinet. Strachey's portrait contains four principal characters: Gladstone, Sir Evelyn Baring (later Lord Cromer), Lord Hartington, and General Gordon. While his portrait of Gladstone is an anthology piece, Strachey nevertheless becomes a little lost in Gladstonian fog. The portrait of Baring was seen to be unjust; Walter Raleigh told Strachey so. Edmund Gosse protested in the *Times Literary Supplement,* and Maurice Baring protested in the *Spectator.*[20] Lord Hartington, in contrast, is presented as the slow man of conscience. While these three portraits take up a few pages each, that of General Gordon pervades the whole study. At the beginning the reader meets Gordon in the Holy

Land in 1883, but then is returned to Gordon's childhood, youth, and his participation in the Crimean War. Strachey follows Gordon through his mission to China, his work at Gravesend and other missions, including his first visit to the Sudan. Then Strachey concentrates upon the Mahdi's rebellion, Gordon's mission to the Sudan, the three characters who, in a sense, decide Gordon's fate, and, finally, Gordon's last days.

Strachey portrays Gordon as an eccentric and as a divided personality; as a man who was at once a man of action and religious speculation.[21] But does this mean that Gordon was necessarily a divided personality? Surely it is possible to be a man of action and a religious thinker without being divided. Strachey, however, presents Gordon as ambitious, speaks of his "deep unconscious instincts", and hints at a homosexuality about which he is not explicit. The issue of Gordon's supposed alcoholism is a vexed one, but it is by no means certain that he was an alcoholic.[22] The constant subject of Strachey's irony is, however, Gordon's religion.[23] It has been noted already that one of the central intentions of *Eminent Victorians* is to mock Victorian religion, and this is done continuously throughout the book.

As noted, Strachey begins this portrait *in medias res* with his eccentric Gordon in the Holy Land in 1883: "This singular person was General Gordon, and his book was the Holy Bible" (189). The soldier with the Bible in his hand is at the center of the bitterly debated, tragic events that Strachey presents as the inevitable product of the strains and tensions of Victorian political life. Where, but in England, he asks, could one find four characters as alike and dissimilar as Mr. Gladstone, Sir Evelyn Baring, Lord Hartington, and General Gordon? These four characters for Strachey "embody the mingling contradictions of the English spirit" (190). Strachey is not simply writing about General Gordon but about "The End of General Gordon," and the other three characters are important for the roles they played in the political drama that issued in Gordon's death. He wants to get behind a controversial historical and political event to consider the human motivations that prompted it.

Strachey indicates that General Gordon was influenced in his religious ideas by his sister Augusta. He was only twenty-one when he went to the Crimea where he behaved with conspicuous gallantry at Sebastopol. In 1860 he was sent to China, and by 1863, when he was only thirty, he was in command of the Ever Victorious Army and was made Companion of the Bath.

In attempting to characterize Gordon on his return to England, Strachey seems to hint at homosexuality:

But he was by nature *farouche*; his soul revolted against dinner–parties and stiff shirts, and the presence of ladies—especially of fashionable ladies—filled him with uneasiness.

. . . . . .

. . . his leisure he devoted to acts of charity and to religious contemplation. The neighbourhood was a poverty-stricken one, and the kind Colonel, with his tripping step and simple manner, was soon a familiar figure in it, chatting with the seamen, taking provisions to starving families, or visiting some bedridden old woman to light her fire. He was particularly fond of boys. Ragged street arabs and rough sailor-lads crowded about him. (197–98)

However, Gordon eludes his biographer, for Strachey has difficulty in understanding the man who gave his Chinese medal to ease the Lancashire famine.

Perhaps, because there is little evidence that Gordon was either homosexual or an alcoholic, Strachey's satire on these subjects is little more than innuendo. On the subject of Gordon's religion, however, Strachey intensifies his attack. What he tries to do in order to diminish Gordon is to identify Gordon's desire to follow the will of God as fatalism. But Strachey does not really know what following the will of God meant to Gordon; he wishes to charge Gordon with ambition for fame and influence but finds himself writing "In the depths of Gordon's soul there were intertwining contradictions—intricate recesses where egoism and renunciation melted into one another, where the flesh lost itself in the spirit, and the spirit in the flesh. What *was* the Will of God?" (200). Strachey appears to be asking as much on his own as on Gordon's account.

He then turns to Gordon's writings in his attempt to reach the heart of his subject's mystery: "The published extracts from these voluminous outpourings lay bare the inner history of Gordon's spirit, and reveal the pious visionary of Gravesend in the restless hero of three continents" (201). But what does this amount to? The reader is confronted once more with a Gordon who wishes to do the will of God, a Gordon who writes, "To be happy, a man must be like a well-broken, willing horse, ready for anything. Events will go as God likes" (201). Again, since the homosexual motivation was tenuous, Strachey tries the alcoholic one. He tries to present Gordon as a man with a Bible and a bottle of brandy: "For months together, we are told, he would drink nothing but pure water; and then . . . water that was not so pure"(203). Strachey's "we are told" is deceptive since he gives us no indication who does the telling apart from himself.

The account of Gordon becomes more confusing than illuminating for two reasons: first, because Gordon was a genuinely complicated personality, and second, because Strachey is unsympathetic to the Christianity that is probably the key to understanding Gordon's personality. Strachey's account is as follows: "And, with these veering moods and dangerous restoratives, there came an intensification of the queer and violent elements in the temper of the man. His eccentricities grew upon him. He found it more and more uncomfortable to follow the ordinary course. Official routine was an agony to him" (203). It is not surprising, then, that when Strachey attempts to account for Gordon's state of mind on his return to England in 1880, he is reduced to questioning, "To what remote corner or what enormous stage, to what self-sacrificing drudgeries or what resounding exploits, would the hand of God lead him now?"(208).

Strachey supplies an account of the Mahdi's power and the political events leading up to Gordon's appointment to the Sudan. He presents a picture of Gordon as a man over fifty who, despite the nickname "Chinese Gordon," was still not widely known. On 7 January 1884 Gordon had been destined to go to the Congo, by 18 January his name was on every tongue as the one man capable of coping with the difficult challenge of the Sudan. He left England "on a mission which was to bring him not only boundless popularity but an immortal fame" (217). Strachey presents Gordon's task as that of an emissary whose responsibility it was to undertake the withdrawal from the Sudan, but he sees Gordon as a man peculiarly unqualified for such a task:

It is difficult to understand what the reasons could have been which induced the Government, not only to override the hesitations of Sir Evelyn Baring, but to overlook the grave and obvious dangers involved in sending such a man as Gordon to the Sudan. The whole history of his life, the whole bent of his character, seemed to disqualify him for the task for which he had been chosen. He was before all things a fighter, an enthusiast, a bold adventurer; and he was now to be entrusted with the conduct of an inglorious retreat. He was alien to the subtleties of civilized statesmanship, he was unamenable to official control, he was incapable of the skilful management of delicate situations; and he was now to be placed in a position of great complexity, requiring at once a cool judgement, a clear perception of fact, and a fixed determination to carry out a line of policy laid down from above. (221)

The tragic ingredients are clearly present for the end of General Gordon. Strachey presents these initially, however, in terms of Gordon's sense of having his ambitions satisfied: "Gordon was in the highest spirits . . . at last he had been entrusted with a task great enough to satisfy even his desires. He was already famous; he would soon be glorious" (228). Gordon entered Khartoum on 8 February 1884. Strachey's sympathy for Gordon quickens as the general moves toward his death. Strachey directs his irony onto the administrative delays that, in fact, destroy Gordon just as in the Florence Nightingale portrait he satirized the bureaucratic bungling of the Crimean War.

In introducing Gladstone, Strachey returns to the animal imagery that he uses throughout *Eminent Victorians*: "The soft serpent coils harden into quick strength" (235). The double-talk of administrative bureaucracy is also used to characterize Gladstone: "General Gordon, he was convinced, might be hemmed in, but he was not surrounded" (237). Gladstone is presented as seeing Gordon selfishly and jealously: "Who was it that was ultimately responsible for sending General Gordon to Khartoum? But then, what did that matter? Why did not the man come back? He was a Christian hero, was he? Were there no other Christian heroes in the world?" (238).

In contrast to the method of presenting Gladstone, Sir Evelyn Baring is presented from General Gordon's point of view: "For him [Gordon] Sir Evelyn Baring was the embodiment of England—or the embodiment of the English official classes, of English diplomacy, of the English government with its hesitations, its insincerities, its double-faced schemes" (239). Sir Evelyn Baring becomes the middleman between Gordon and the British government who abets Gordon's destruction. Gordon rises in our sympathy (and Strachey's) as Gladstone and then Baring are introduced: "On one side of him was a veering and vacillating Government; on the other, a frenzied enthusiast. It was his [Baring's] business to interpret to the first the wishes, or rather the inspirations, of the second, and to convey to the second the decisions, or rather the indecisions, of the first" (241). Yet from April until September, Baring was at a financial conference in London. Meanwhile Gordon's sense of his mission grew in strength. The people of Khartoum saw the Mahdi as a false Mahdi and put their trust in the

Governor-General. So "How could he desert his people? It was impossible. It would be, as he himself exclaimed in one of his latest telegrams to Sir Evelyn Baring, 'the climax of meanness,' even to contemplate such an act" (244). Gordon's situation was, indeed, dire. "He seemed to be utterly abandoned. Sir Evelyn Baring had disappeared into his financial conference. In England Mr. Gladstone had held firm, had outfaced the House of Commons, had ignored the Press. He appeared to have triumphed" (245).

At this point Strachey introduces Lord Hartington whose "conscience was of a piece with the rest of him. It was not, like Mr. Gladstone's, a salamander-conscience—an intangible, dangerous creature, that loved to live in the fire; nor was it, like Gordon's, a restless conscience; nor, like Sir Evelyn Baring's, a diplomatic conscience; it was a commonplace affair" (245). Lord Hartington is characterized as stolid and dull. Strachey's conclusion is that, "The fate of General Gordon . . . —was finally determined by the fact that Lord Hartington was slow" (247). He sees Lord Hartington as a machine moving "—surely, firmly, completely, in the best English manner, and too late" (247).

Although the popular song about Gordon runs:

> Too late! Too late to save him,
> In vain, in vain they tried.
> His life was England's glory,
> His death was England's pride.

Strachey identifies Hartington's slowness with the nation's—a nation that was, in fact, outraged by the news of Gordon's death as was its queen. The English people saw Lord Hartington as a man of honesty and integrity. The tragic irony of Gordon's end resulted, in part, from the lateness of Hartington's insistence upon a relief force being sent to Khartoum.

As he depicts Gordon alone in Khartoum, there is a rush of personal sympathy and identification on Strachey's part. He says that "There are passages in the *Khartoum Journals* which call up in a flash the light, gliding figure, and the blue eyes with the candour of childhood still shining in them; one can almost hear the low voice, the singularly distinct articulation, the persuasive—the self-persuasive—sentences, following each other so unassumingly between the puffs of a cigarette"(251). Indeed, Strachey writes of Gordon's *Journals* in a way that reminds the reader of Strachey's own letters. His identification with his suffering subject is almost complete:

A more singular set of state papers was never compiled. Sitting there, in the solitude of his palace, with ruin closing round him, with anxieties on every hand, with doom hanging above his head, he let his pen rush on for hour after hour in an ecstasy of communication, a tireless unburdening of the spirit. (250–251)

Anyone who has read Strachey's letters to Duncan Grant or to his brother James will find them described in these words. Strachey tells the reader that Gordon "drew caricatures, in the margin, of Sir Evelyn Baring, with sentences of shocked pomposity coming out of his mouth" (252).

The last months of Gordon's life are described by Strachey with copious quotations from Gordon's *Journals* and letters. Here he does catch, at last, the defiant independence, what he calls the "contradictious" character of Gordon, " 'if any emissary or letter comes up here ordering me to come down, I WILL NOT OBEY IT, BUT WILL STAY HERE, AND FALL WITH TOWN, AND RUN ALL RISKS.' This was sheer insubordination, no doubt; but he could not help that; it was not in his nature to be obedient. 'I know if *I* was chief, I would never employ *myself,* for I am incorrigible.' " (253).

Doing his duty, as he told his sister, and following the example of his beloved Christ, Gordon simply continued until the end. " 'I shall never (D.V.)' he had told Sir Evelyn Baring, 'be taken alive' " (263). In his presentation of Gordon's death, Strachey waxes a little biblically melodramatic:

Then it is said that Taha Shahin, the Dongolawi, cried in a loud voice "Mala' oun el yom yomek!" (O cursèd one, your time is come), and plunged his spear into the Englishman's body. His only reply was a gesture of contempt. Another spear transfixed him; he fell, and the swords of three other Dervishes instantly hacked him to death. Thus, if we are to believe the official chroniclers, in the dignity of unresisting disdain, General Gordon met his end. (264)

Gordon's head was taken to the Mahdi. The nation was outraged, and the Queen wrote a letter of sympathy to Gordon's sister who in return sent the Queen her brother's Bible. Six months later the Mahdi himself died. In concluding his portrait Strachey returns to his characteristi-

cally ironic manner: "Every one agreed that General Gordon had been
avenged at last. Who could doubt it? General Gordon himself, possi-
bly, fluttering, in some remote Nirvana, the pages of a phantasmal
Bible, might have ventured a satirical remark" (266).

"The End of General Gordon" is certainly the most moving portrait
in *Eminent Victorians*. It contains a tension that the portrait of Dr.
Arnold lacks but that is also present in the portrait of Florence Nightingale. Strachey's twin intentions in *Eminent Victorians* had been to unmask Victorian hypocrisy and renew the art of biography. The second
intention was more successfully accomplished than the first, though
Eminent Victorians is certainly the liveliest and most controversial of
Strachey's works. It is natural that this work springs most immediately
to mind when Lytton Strachey's name is mentioned. Its reputation,
too, has endured beyond the reputation of his other works.

Chapter Four

The Biographer: *Queen Victoria* (1921) and *Books and Characters* (1922)

Queen Victoria

In his biography of Queen Victoria Lytton Strachey departs in important ways from his practice in *Eminent Victorians*. *Queen Victoria* is a more scholarly work than *Eminent Victorians* as Strachey states in his preface: "Authority for every important statement of fact in the following pages will be found in the footnotes." There are no footnotes in *Eminent Victorians*. The irony and satire in *Eminent Victorians* are mellowed in *Queen Victoria* to comedy and humor. Strachey's change of tone reflects the changed circumstances of his life which, by the time of his writing *Queen Victoria*, had become more settled and domestic. World War I was over, and Strachey was in every way more secure. *Eminent Victorians*, despite its iconoclasm, had been a success and had given him prominence in the social as well as the literary world. He was entering middle age, and the rebellious strain was no longer as strong in him as it had been when he was writing *Eminent Victorians*.

Queen Victoria had to be more circumstantial and sustain a continuous narrative in a way that had not always been necessary in *Eminent Victorians*. Strachey begins his biography by discussing Queen Victoria's antecedents. Then, he opens the second chapter, "Childhood," in a deliberately low-keyed fashion: "The child who, in these not very impressive circumstances, appeared in the world, received but scant attention."[1] When Victoria's grandfather's (George III's) death was followed by that of her father, Strachey tells us that "She alone stood between the country and her terrible uncle, the Duke of Cumberland" (23). The little girl is thereby given an awesome role.

Throughout the biography Strachey presents Victoria as a tiny woman confronting an enormous responsibility. The frequent comment that Strachey came to criticize but remained to admire Victoria is justified. Though he pokes fun at her ordinariness, he cannot help but sympathize with and be moved by the overwhelming burden that she is required to bear. Hence, the reader finds the kind of tension already noted in the portraits of Florence Nightingale and General Gordon in which Strachey's impulse to satirize is blunted by his reluctant acknowledgment of the strength and achievement of his subject. The weight of narrative detail is a further factor in blunting the edge of the satire that Strachey had favored in *Eminent Victorians*. His historical training begins to assert itself with the necessity to sketch in a good deal of the political and historical background of Victoria's life.

When Strachey comes to comment on Victoria's education, he connects her mother's educational ideas with those of Dr. Arnold. The extent of his modification of his satiric manner should be noted, for the hostility to Dr. Arnold evident in *Eminent Victorians* is quite diminished here: "Her educational conceptions were those of Dr. Arnold, whose views were just then beginning to permeate society. Dr. Arnold's object was first and foremost, to make his pupils 'in the highest and truest sense of the words, Christian gentlemen'; intellectual refinements might follow. The Duchess felt convinced that it was her supreme duty in life to make quite sure that her daughter should grow up into a Christian queen" (28–29). Perhaps a desire to placate his mother, who was originally apprehensive about his writing a biography of Queen Victoria,[2] also led Strachey to curb his satiric impulse.

Throughout the work Strachey paints a picture of a Victoria incompetent in practical matters (like Strachey himself), a Victoria who always relied on fatherly men to support her (Melbourne, Albert, Disraeli, John Brown), rather as Strachey and Carrington depended on Ralph Partridge to drive them about and buy their rail tickets. But Strachey sees Victoria's early life as dominated by female influence, rather as his own was. In both these instances the biographer seems to project his own concerns and experience onto his subject. He notes that during Victoria's early life "her spirit . . . was hardly reached by those two great influences, without which no growing life can truly prosper— humor and imagination" (33). So it is not so much a question of Strachey changing his attitude to Victoria during the course of the book as his appearing sympathetic to her from the beginning. He speaks of Victoria's journal, which she began at the age of thirteen, and of the influence of her governess, Baroness Lehzen, who was the daughter of a German pastor: "The young creature that one sees there, self-depicted in ingenuous clarity, with her sincerity, her simplicity, her quick affections and pious resolutions, might almost have been the daughter of a German pastor herself" (33).

Strachey makes a point of calling attention to an early meeting with her cousin Albert who was to have the most profound influence upon her life. However, Strachey's saccharine and external characterization of Victoria's early feeling for Albert scarcely does it justice (38). For the most part Strachey sees Victoria in childhood as a victim of intrigues and political conflicts that were beyond her. In relation to these events he presents Victoria as "shut away in the seclusion of Kensington, a small, unknown figure, lost in the large shadow of her mother's domination" (47).

Victoria's sole support at this point, Strachey suggests, is King Leopold II who advises her " 'to be courageous, firm, and honest, as you have been till now' " (48). At the close of the chapter, when Strachey describes the death of William IV, it is clear that even the antireligious satire that dominated *Eminent Victorians* has been tempered in *Queen Victoria*.

In part, the biography is built upon Victoria's relationships to the men in her life. In the third chapter Strachey presents her relationship with Lord Melbourne. Her dependence upon male guidance is shown as springing from her early isolation and exclusion from male company. Her uncles are seen as wintry and Victoria herself as a new spring. Her continuous need for male guidance (at least as Strachey sees the matter) is revealed in her early relationship with King Leopold. In this connection Strachey shows the predominance of King Leopold's envoy Baron Stockmar: "The Baron's secret skill had given Leopold his unexceptionable kingdom; and Leopold, in his turn, as time went on, was able to furnish the Baron with more and more keys to more and more back doors" (58). Like a dramatist preparing for the entrance of a hero, Strachey has presented these influences in order to intensify the sense of Melbourne's eclipsing them. So Strachey writes in his characteristically exaggerated and melodramatic manner:

> With Lehzen to supervise every detail of her conduct, with Stockmar in the next room, so full of wisdom and experience of affairs, with her Uncle Leopold's letters, too, pouring out so constantly their stream of encouragements, general reflections, and highly valuable tips, Victoria even had she been without other guidance, would have stood in no lack of private counsellors. But other guidance she had; for all these influences paled before a new star, of the first magnitude, which, rising suddenly upon her horizon, immediately dominated her life. (59)

Strachey certainly presents the new star as attractively as possible: "William Lamb, Viscount Melbourne, was fifty-eight years of age, and had been for the last three years Prime Minister of England. . . . His mind, at once supple and copious, his temperament, at once calm and sensitive, enabled him not merely to work but to live with perfect facility and with the grace of strength" (59–60). Using the seasonal imagery that runs through the book, Strachey presents Melbourne as "an autumn rose" (63).

Beyond this, he continues the psychological method of character analysis begun in *Eminent Victorians*. So he says of Melbourne, "The feminine element in him made it . . . natural and inevitable for him to be the friend of a great many women; but the masculine element in him was strong as well" (64). In the forward movement of a style that depends on accumulation and repetition, Strachey tries to carry the romance of Melbourne's past into his relations with Victoria in the present:

The man of the world who had been the friend of Byron and the Regent, . . . the lover whose soft words had captivated such beauty and such passion and such wit, might now be seen, evening after evening, talking with infinite politeness to a schoolgirl, bolt upright, amid the silence and rigidity of Court etiquette. (65)

In such a way the Regency becomes the Victorian period and Strachey tries to capture the transition here.

Strachey was now a literary success and it was, perhaps, with at least half an eye on the popular market that he produced the romantic writing evident in his account of Victoria and Melbourne's relationship: "The light of the morning is upon it; and, in the rosy radiance, the figure of 'Lord M.' emerges, glorified and supreme. If she is the heroine of the story, he is the hero" (67). This may account for Strachey's irritation when Virginia Woolf asked him, perhaps a little jealously, what it was like to be a success.[3]

Queen Victoria's dependence on Melbourne was perceived to be so great that Strachey notes, " 'Mrs. Melbourne' was shouted at her when she appeared at her balcony" (91). Of Melbourne he writes, "The springs of his sensibility, hidden deep within him, were overflowing. Often as he bent over her hand and kissed it, he found himself in tears" (92). For her part it is only the relationship with Albert that breaks the spell of the relation to Melbourne.

Always interested in historical change and in points of transition in cultural and social history, Strachey presents Victoria's attachment to Melbourne as a nostalgia for the eighteenth-century, a nostalgia that Strachey felt strongly himself because of his family's roots in that century: "For a moment the child of a new age looked back, and wavered towards the eighteenth century. It was the most critical moment of her career. Had those influences lasted, the development of her character, the history of her life, would have been completely changed" (93).

The fourth and pivotal chapter of the biography is called "Marriage," and Strachey indicates immediately that Albert was always intended to marry his "little English May flower" (97). The marriage is engineered by Baron Stockmar. Adhering to the pattern already discussed of presenting Victoria in relation to the men in her life, Strachey presents Albert in deliberate contrast to Melbourne. Some of the irony of *Eminent Victorians* remains: "Intelligent and painstaking, he had been touched by the moral earnestness of his generation; at the age of eleven he surprised his father by telling him that he hoped to make himself 'a good and useful man' " (98). Unhappily, some of the capacity for falsification noted, particularly in the portrait of Dr. Arnold, in *Eminent Victorians*, remains as well. Thus, Strachey writes of Albert that "owing either to his peculiar upbringing or to a more fundamental idiosyncrasy he had a marked distaste for the opposite sex . . . and though, later on, he grew more successful in disguising such feelings, the feelings remained" (99). Prince Albert's most recent biographer, Robert Rhodes James, denies any suggestion that Albert was homosexual and says that Strachey is merely retailing the gossip of the Countess of Bedford in implying that Albert did not love Victoria.[4] Strachey writes that when Albert married Victoria, "He would not be there to please himself, but for a very different purpose—to do good" (105).

Lord Melbourne was replaced as prime minister by Sir Robert Peel and later the Duke of Wellington. Victoria's antipathy to these men is seen by Strachey as a reason for her increasing dependence on Albert. Another reason Strachey notes is that Baroness Lehzen, whose influence over the young Victoria had been so considerable, now retired to Bückeburg. Paradoxically, considering Strachey's implications about Albert's sexual nature, his power over Victoria is presented in embarrassingly sexual terms: "Time and the pressure of inevitable circumstances were for him; every day his predominance grew more assured—and every night" (121–22).

Without experience of married life himself, though sensing something of its happiness, perhaps through his relationship with Carrington, Strachey tends to melodramatize Victoria's situation though he manages to capture a partial sense of her joy in marriage: "The early discords had passed away completely—resolved into the absolute harmony of married life" (122). He continues a little ironically, "In Victoria's eyes, life had become an idyll, and, if the essential elements of an idyll are happiness, love and simplicity, an idyll it was; though, indeed, it was of a kind that might have disconcerted Theocritus" (123). The contrast between the heavy cynicism of *Eminent Victorians* and the light irony found here should be noted.

By posing questions Strachey attempts to dramatize Victoria's inner life: "How did she know? What is the distinction between happiness that is real and happiness that is felt? So a philosopher—Lord M. himself perhaps—might have inquired. But she was no philosopher, and Lord M. was a phantom, and Albert was beside her, and that was enough" (124). Victoria is presented, then, as finding her fullest satisfaction in Albert's love. However, Strachey goes on to depict the relationship between Victoria and Albert as somewhat one-sided: "Victoria idolised him; but it was understanding that he craved for, not idolatry" (129).

Once Albert enters the scene there is a noticeable transfer of authorial allegiance to him. Strachey identifies with the overworked, mysogynistic Albert of his imagination. "What more and more absorbed him—bringing with it a comfort of its own—was his work" (130). Then Strachey notes the growth of Albert's power: "He had become the Queen's Private Secretary, her confidential adviser, her second self. He was now always present at her interviews with Ministers" (136). Strachey shows how, through Albert's pervasive influence, Victoria, who had earlier hated Sir Robert Peel, comes to respect him. He notes that Albert's influence was exercised so subtly that it was scarcely noticeable, but nonetheless, "by the close of Peel's administration, Albert had become, in effect, the King of England" (137).

With the arrival of six children and removal to Osborne on the Isle of Wight, Victoria and Albert, in Strachey's view, created a family life that became a model for the national life. The transition that Strachey earlier depicted in process when Albert replaced Melbourne as the dominant influence in Victoria's life, is now shown to be complete: "The last vestige of the eighteenth century had disappeared; cynicism and subtlety were shrivelled into powder; and duty, industry, morality, and domesticity triumphed over them. Even the very chairs and tables had assumed, with a singular responsiveness, the forms of prim solidity. The Victorian Age was in full swing" (141–42). It is certainly possible to sense, here, at least an undercurrent of the irony that dominated *Eminent Victorians*. Strachey depicts The Great Exhibition of 1851 as the culminating event of Victoria and Albert's life together. Its opening on 1 May was, Strachey tells us, the happiest day of Victoria's life. The Exhibition was designed to be "an international monument to those supreme blessings of civilisation—peace, progress, and prosperity" (142).

In chapter 5, "Lord Palmerston," Strachey further develops Albert's predominance. Yet here he indicates that Albert is himself controlled by Baron Stockmar. Strachey shows how the influence of Stockmar on Albert and Albert on Victoria leads to a conflict between the Queen and her government when Albert's views of British foreign policy differ from Lord Palmerston's. When Palmerston resigns, Albert is blamed. Strachey suggests that the people of Britain are intensely suspicious of foreigners and notes "Decidedly, there were elements in the situation which went far to justify popular alarm. A foreign Baron controlled a foreign Prince, and the foreign Prince controlled the Crown of England" (183–84). The characteristic use of repetition in the final sentence, here, creates a sense of the depths of political intrigue that Strachey frequently evokes throughout *Queen Victoria*. Albert's dominant role in Victoria's life is the reason that he dominates the center of Strachey's biography of Victoria.

Strachey presents the difficulties and unhappiness that Victoria and Albert suffer in their relationship with the Prince of Wales, whom Strachey portrays as more interested in frivolity than in work. However, he indicates that Victoria's lease of Balmoral House in 1848 and the pleasure that she and Albert enjoy in their Scottish residence to some degree offsets this unhappiness.

Albert's death, which is described in chapter 6, "Last Years of the Prince Consort," is shown as caused in part by his obsession with work, which Strachey sees as morbid. This health-destroying addiction is noted in Strachey's comment that "Between 1853 and 1857 fifty folio volumes were filled with the comments of his pen upon the Eastern question" (197). Albert's work obsession is portrayed as becoming suicidal: "His industry grew almost maniacal. . . . His very recreations became duties. He enjoyed himself by time-table" (210). Albert's fatal illness, in fact, began in November 1861, and Strachey records how by early December, "The restlessness and the acute suffering of the earlier

days gave place to a settled torpor and an ever-deepening gloom" (215).
Strachey's account of Victoria's response to Albert's death on 14 Decem-
ber seems to be colored by his own hysteria and skepticism: "She
shrieked—one long wild shriek that ran through the terror-stricken
Castle—and understood that she had lost him for ever" (217). Baron
Stockmar's death followed only eighteen months later.

The account of Victoria's response to Albert's death that opens
Strachey's seventh chapter, "Widowhood," provides an explanation for
the imbalance in the biography in favor of the first half of Victoria's
life:

The death of the Prince Consort was the central turning-point in the history of
Queen Victoria. She herself felt that her true life had ceased with her husband's, and that the remainder of her days upon earth was of a twilight
nature—an epilogue to a drama that was done. (218)

Strachey notes that the "great and varied quantity of authentic information" that had illuminated the first forty-two years of Victoria's life is
absent for the later years. The reader must therefore, according to
Strachey, "be content . . . with a brief and summary relation" (218).
Six chapters of *Queen Victoria* are devoted to the first forty years of her
life and four to the last forty.

Strachey gives an indication of the depth of Victoria's devastation at
Albert's death when he quotes from a letter she wrote to King Leopold:
" 'The poor fatherless baby of eight months . . . is now the utterly
crushed and heart-broken widow of forty-two' " (222). In offering this
quotation, which links her feelings of desolation and helplessness on
her husband's death with her state as an orphaned infant, Strachey
emphasizes both the fact of and the reason for her lifelong dependence
on father figures.

Almost in contradiction to this emphasis, Strachey suggests that
Victoria's tone challenges the will of God: "The tone of outraged Maj-
esty seems to be discernible. Did she wonder in her heart of hearts how
the Deity could have dared?" (222) In keeping with this suggestion, he
characterizes Victoria's feelings for Albert as going beyond human love
when he writes with characteristic accumulative repetition, "all other
emotions gave way before her overmastering determination to con-
tinue, absolutely unchanged for the rest of her life on earth, her reverence, her obedience, her idolatry" (222).

Of Victoria's widowhood Strachey notes, "As the years passed her depression seemed to deepen and her loneliness to grow more intense" (224). His effort to characterize this state leads to strained writing betrayed by the crass alliteration of the following sentence: "It was not mere sorrow that kept her so strangely sequestered; it was devotion, it was self-immolation; it was the laborious legacy of love" (230). Victoria's life, he records, became increasingly devoted to preserving Albert's memory. He tells us that Albert's speeches, edited by Sir Arthur Helps, appeared in 1862, General Grey wrote a biography of his early years, and between 1874 and 1880 Theodore Martin's five-volume biography appeared. The Poet Laureate was pressed into service, the Frogmore mausoleum was built, and statues were erected at Aberdeen, Perth, and Wolverhampton. Work was begun on Gilbert Scott's Albert Memorial and Hall in May 1864. The hall was opened in July 1872 but it was four years more before the central figure for the memorial was ready. Strachey notes that "The statue was of bronze gilt and weighed nearly ten tons" (239). He seems to imply that it expressed the weight of Victoria's grief.

Luckily, Lord Beaconsfield appeared to restore the queen to something like spirits. Chapter 8, "Mr. Gladstone and Lord Beaconsfield," presents the ascendancy of yet another father figure in Victoria's life. Strachey writes that Lord Clarendon claimed that Disraeli addressed the queen in "his best novel style," (242). He also records Disraeli's famous piece of flattery, "we authors, ma'am" (243). Disraeli, in fact, rose in Victoria's favor in contrast to his political opponent, Gladstone, of whom Strachey notes that "The well-known complaint—'He speaks to me as if I were a public meeting'—whether authentic or no—and the turn of the sentence is surely a little too epigrammatic to be genuinely Victorian—undoubtedly expresses the essential element of her antipathy" (246–47).

In presenting Disraeli's relationship with Victoria, Strachey highlights its importance in her later life with the claim: "If Victoria had died in the early seventies, there can be little doubt that the voice of the world would have pronounced her a failure" (251). In 1874, however, the Liberals were routed and a period of Tory supremacy began: "Then there followed six years of excitement, of enchantment, of felicity, of glory, of romance. The amazing being, who now at last, at the age of seventy, after a lifetime of extraordinary struggles, had turned into reality the absurdest of his boyhood's dreams, knew well enough how to

make his own, with absolute completeness, the heart of the Sovereign
Lady whose servant, and whose master, he had so miraculously become"
(252).

Strachey uses romance and theatrical language in depicting the relationship between Disraeli and Victoria. He even presents Disraeli as
attending his own consummate performance. Disraeli's personal name
for Victoria "The Faery" gives the whole episode the aura of theatrical
romance. Hence the Oriental characterization that Strachey gives Disraeli: "The smile hovered and vanished, and, bowing low with Oriental
gravity and Oriental submissiveness, he set himself to his task" (253).
The Orient has always had romance and magical associations in English
literature. Strachey indicates that Disraeli boasted of his flattery to
Matthew Arnold, "You have heard me called a flatterer . . . and it is
true. Everyone likes flattery; and when you come to royalty you should
lay it on with a trowel" (254). Strachey handles this with a curiously
fastidious irony: "In those expert hands the trowel seemed to assume
the qualities of some lofty masonic symbol—to be the ornate and
glittering vehicle of verities unrealised by the profane" (255).

Strachey shows the beneficial effects of Disraeli's personality on Victoria: "she expanded to the rays of Disraeli's devotion like a flower in the
sun" (257). He also notes that Victoria was in some measure attracted
to "The strain of charlatanism" (257) in men like Napoleon III and
Disraeli. Under Disraeli's influence, Strachey notes, "she completely
regained the self-confidence which had been slipping away from her
throughout the dark period that followed Albert's death" (257).

Strachey speculates about Disraeli's character to which he as much as
Victoria seems to be attracted: "Actor and spectator both, the two
characters were so intimately blended together in that odd composition
that they formed an inseparable unity, and it was impossible to say that
one of them was less genuine than the other" (260). Strachey seems to
find his own sense of division healed in the image of Disraeli's blending
of two selves.

In spite of the personal rapport between Victoria and Disraeli,
Strachey shows that Disraeli sometimes had difficulty in controlling
Victoria in matters of government policy. However, even when Victo-
ria and Disraeli are in conflict, Strachey continues to use his Arabian
Nights imagery to describe their relationship, in this instance seeing
Victoria as a genie whom Disraeli "had rashly called out of her bottle,
and who was now intent upon showing her supernal power" (267).
Strachey throws a literary veil over the human reality of their relation-

ship and presents it as an elaborate game. No doubt this was to some extent true, but it cannot have been the whole story.

Chapter 9 of *Queen Victoria* is called "Old Age." With Leopold's death in 1865 and Disraeli's in 1881, Victoria lost two of the male supports to her widowed existence. They were replaced by John Brown who had been Albert's servant at Balmoral. Pointing out how important John Brown became to Victoria, Strachey notes that "She allowed him to take liberties with her which would have been unthinkable from anybody else." He continues, "upon somebody she longed to depend. Her days were heavy with the long process of domination" (272). In fact, Strachey has shown Victoria's life as a "long process" of dependence, although her domination, particularly of the Prince of Wales, is noted. Dependence and domination are closely allied.

Strachey sees the relationship with John Brown as a means of maintaining connection with Albert: "She came to believe at last—or so it appeared—that the spirit of Albert was nearer when Brown was near" (273). However, Strachey's treatment of the relationship between mistress and servant is not without irony. He mentions Brown's "too acute appreciation of Scotch whisky" but then adds in ironic palliation, "But he served his mistress faithfully, and to ignore him would be a sign of disrespect in her biographer" (273). The irony persists when Strachey adds "and yet—such is the world!—there were those who actually treated the relations between their sovereign and her servant as a theme for ribald jests" (274). There is certainly the sense that Strachey has his tongue in his cheek here.

Strachey notes the other losses that Victoria suffered after Albert's death in 1861: Princess Alice, her daughter, died in 1878, Disraeli in 1881, John Brown in 1883, and her son Prince Leopold, Duke of Albany, in 1884. Besides this, he catalogs the seven assassination attempts that Victoria suffered between 1840 and 1882. In chronicling Victoria's later life he speaks of how she and her people were at one in their outrage over General Gordon's death in 1885. The following year "she opened in high state the Colonial and Indian Exhibition" (280).

The year 1887 was, of course, the year of the Golden Jubilee. The reader becomes aware that Strachey is now writing of a period that he actually experienced in his childhood and youth. Rather exaggeratedly, though, he writes: "The solid splendour of the decade between Victoria's two jubilees can hardly be paralleled in the annals of England" (281). There is an undercurrent of irony, however, that recalls Froude's portmanteaus in *Eminent Victorians* when he writes of Victoria that "she was a part of the establishment—an essential part as it seemed—a fixture—a magnificent, immoveable sideboard in the huge saloon of state" (281). The image, however ironic, does point to the fact that Victoria had, for many of her subjects, ceased to be a person and had become an icon or national institution.

More seriously, Strachey suggests that Victoria discovers a belated maturity in old age that frees her from dependence and allows her to draw strength from herself. "Her being, revolving for so many years round an external object, now changed its motion and found its centre in itself" (282). He notes that she was the dominating figure in her large family. She had thirty-seven great-grandchildren at the time of her death. And the Prince of Wales still quailed before his mother when he was over fifty years of age. Even so, Strachey shows that Victoria remained obsessed with the memory of her dead husband to an astonishing degree: "every bed in which Victoria slept had attached to it, at the back, on the right-hand side, above the pillow, a photograph of the head and shoulders of Albert as he lay dead, surmounted by a wreath of immortelles" (294–95). For forty years following his death (until Victoria herself died), Albert's clothes were laid out every day and water was set ready for him.

At this point in his portrait, Strachey looks at Victoria's interests and attitudes, at the ways in which she reflected her time and the ways in which she differed from it. For example, despite great turmoil in religious life in England during her reign, and despite her position as head of the Church of England, Victoria, "seemed to feel most at home in the simple faith of the Presbyterian Church of Scotland" (298). Strachey sees Victoria's attention to goodness, duty, conscience, and morality as expressing her age: "The middle classes, firm in the triple brass of their respectability, rejoiced with a special joy over the most respectable of Queens" (304). He also points out that where Albert had a thorough understanding of the industrial development of the age, and an appreciation of advances in science, Victoria herself was not interested in either. Strachey goes on to note that Victoria, ironically since she was herself a powerful woman, opposed the movement for the emancipation of women, which she called "this mad, wicked folly of 'Woman's Rights' " (299). On a minor note, he points out that Victoria was completely opposed to smoking.

As if to contrast Albert's power to Victoria's weakness, Strachey says that "From 1840 to 1861 the power of the Crown steadily increased in

England; from 1861 to 1901 it steadily declined" (300). Victoria received high praise for acquiescing in this political development, but Strachey believes that she never properly understood the implications of this change and that if she had, she would have been most displeased. He obviously savors the irony of this situation.

Strachey sees Victoria's character as one in which obstinacy would give way at the last moment to compliance. Because of this, he believes that "it happened that while by the end of the reign the power of the sovereign had appreciably diminished, the prestige of the sovereign had enormously grown" (303). "For one thing, she was of a great age—an almost indispensable qualification for popularity in England. . . . She had reigned for sixty years, and she was not out" (303). Here, in Strachey's hands, Victoria seems to have metamorphosed from a sideboard to a cricketer.

In explaining the reasons for Victoria's popularity Strachey then focuses on her writing. He points out that "Her utterly unliterary style has at least the merit of being a vehicle exactly suited to her thoughts and feelings; and even the platitude of her phraseology carries with it a curiously personal flavour. Undoubtedly it was through her writings that she touched the heart of the public" (305). Strachey is surely honest in admitting his own response as he notes, "They felt instinctively Victoria's irresistible sincerity, and they responded. And in truth it was an endearing trait" (305).

As time went on Strachey found himself increasingly nostalgic about the period in which he had been born. So, after mentioning the Jubilee of 1897, his moving depiction of Victoria at the end of her life almost sounds as though he were writing a tribute to his mother who had felt doubtful about her son attempting such a biography: "The girl, the wife, the aged woman, were the same: vitality, conscientiousness, pride, and simplicity were hers to the latest hour" (306).

This direct, recapitulatory sentence prepares the way for the famous, anthologized final paragraph of the short tenth chapter, "The End":

When, two days previously, the news of the approaching end had been made public, astonished grief had swept over the country. It appeared as if some monstrous reversal of the course of nature was about to take place. The vast majority of her subjects had never known a time when Queen Victoria had not been reigning over them. She had become an indissoluble part of their whole scheme of things, and that they were about to lose her appeared a scarcely possible thought. She herself, as she lay blind and silent, seemed to those who watched her to be divested of all thinking—to have glided already, unawares, into oblivion. Yet, perhaps, in the secret chambers of consciousness, she had her thoughts, too. Perhaps her fading mind called up once more the shadows of the past to float before it, and retraced, for the last time, the vanished visions of that long history—passing back and back, through the cloud of years, to older and even older memories—to the spring woods at Osborne, so full of primroses for Lord Beaconsfield—to Lord Palmerston's queer clothes and high demeanour, and Albert's face under the green lamp, and Albert's first stag at Balmoral, and Albert in his blue and silver uniform, and the Baron coming in through a doorway, and Lord M. dreaming at Windsor with the rooks cawing in the elm-trees, and the Archbishop of Canterbury on his knees in the dawn, and the old King's turkey-cock ejaculations, and Uncle Leopold's soft voice at Claremont, and Lehzen with the globes, and her mother's feathers sweeping down towards her, and a great old repeater-watch of her father's in its tortoise-shell case, and a yellow rug, and some friendly flounces of sprigged muslin, and the trees and the grass of Kensington. (309–10)

Essentially, Strachey's technique in this famous passage is to take Virginia Woolf's stream-of-consciousness method and make it accessible to a wider audience than Woolf herself commanded. Significantly, *Queen Victoria* is dedicated to Virginia Woolf. In effect, Strachey ties up the strands of his narrative in this last purple passage, and brings his work full circle from death back to birth, sweeping Victoria back through her life as she lies on her deathbed. Strachey loved deathbed scenes. There are many throughout his biographies, but this is the most famous, just as it is the best-known passage in his work. While Strachey is understandably best known for *Eminent Victorians, Queen Victoria* is the high point of his achievement, the work in which he attained maturity. This last paragraph is lyrical rather than ironic, and Strachey shows here his capacity to develop a poetic prose that he would attempt to make the overall vehicle of his last full-length work, *Elizabeth and Essex*.

At the opening of the paragraph, however, one sees his characteristic propensity to overwrite, the adjectival inclination in "astonished grief," "monstrous reversal," and "vast majority," as if Strachey only feels confident of gaining attention if he exaggerates. This continues into "indissoluble part," "whole scheme of things," and "scarcely possible thought." It is, in truth, a kind of flashy journalese, the sort of writing for which the *Daily Express* was later to become infamous. But as Strachey moves from outer to inner, from the public response to the news of Victoria's approaching death to his attempt to represent Victoria's own thoughts, the writing becomes more subtle and imaginative. "Blind and silent" characterizes the queen on her deathbed realistically and well. The repeated "perhaps" in "Yet, perhaps, in the secret chambers of consciousness, she had her thoughts, too. Perhaps her fading mind called up once more the shadows of the past to float before it" provides an honest acknowledgment that Strachey is making an effort of imagination rather than presenting what actually occurred. There is a sympathetic effort on his part to imagine Victoria's inner thoughts at the time of death, and also to review her life in order to provide an appropriate coda to his biography.

This effort of reminiscence that sweeps the reader gently back through Victoria's life has a pleasantly lyrical and nostalgic effect. The repetitions of "back and back" and "older and even older" create an almost Tennysonian poetic prose. Yet this is some of Strachey's most subtle writing. At first the memories of people are external: "primroses for Lord Beaconsfield," "Lord Palmerston's queer clothes and high demeanour," "Albert's first stag at Balmoral, and Albert in his blue and silver uniform." The conjunctions, nevertheless, help to establish the lyrical flow, but as the reader returns to Victoria's childhood, he is also returned by degrees to a more inward perspective. This is what moves the reader to identify with Victoria presented simultaneously in death and at the beginning of life. It would be wrong to call the writing tragic but it is certainly elegiac and movingly so.

From the Baron in the doorway the reader moves to "Lord M. dreaming at Windsor with the rooks cawing in the elm-trees," himself a figure of age here, to "the Archbishop of Canterbury on his knees in the dawn," an image that suggests both death and birth yet is also connected to Victoria's accession and marriage. Then the images shift from the frighteningly animal to the reassuringly human seen from Victoria's point of view, from the alien "old King's turkey-cock ejaculations" to "Uncle Leopold's soft voice at Claremont." In the last words of the paragraph the reader is reminded of the earliest objects Victoria would have remembered, of the people closest to her in her earliest moments, and finally of the natural world into which she was born. The whole movement of the passage has sought simultaneously to represent Victoria's death but also to review her life from her point of view. The reader sees her in death once more as a little child. Strachey tries to give his biography the symmetry of a work of art that will also offer a final image of Victoria. A reader of Virginia Woolf is reminded of Lilly

Briscoe completing her painting in *To The Lighthouse:* "and Lehzen with
the globes and her mother's feathers sweeping down towards her, and a
great old repeater-watch of her father's in its tortoiseshell case, and a
yellow rug, and some friendly flounces of sprigged muslin, and the
trees and grass at Kensington." Of course, the deathbed scene is something that had become very popular in the Victorian age itself: consider, for example, Dickens's death of Little Nell, Robert Browning's
"The Bishop Orders His Tomb," Emily Brontë's death of Heathcliff, or
Kipling's "The Mary Gloster." So, although Strachey's method of treatment is modernist, stream of consciousness, the deathbed scene itself is
more traditional and appropriate to the subject that Strachey is
treating—Queen Victoria herself.

Books and Characters (1922)

In 1922 Strachey published a selection of his essays and reviews
called *Books and Characters: French and English.* It was dedicated to John
Maynard Keynes. Some of these pieces have already been discussed in
chapter 2. The purpose of the publication of this selection at this time
seems to have been to consolidate his reputation following the success
of *Eminent Victorians* and *Queen Victoria.*

The volume begins with the essay "Racine" (1908), which is probably Strachey's finest contribution to literary criticism. In it he argues
that Racine has never been properly appreciated in England yet deserves
to be. It is understandably the first piece in the volume. This is
followed by three pieces on English topics: "Sir Thomas Browne"
(1906), "Shakespeare's Final Period" (1906), and "The Lives of the
Poets" (1906). The first of these defends the ornate prose style of Sir
Thomas Browne, and argues that Dr. Johnson, in fact, returned to
Browne to strengthen English prose. The second piece suggests that
Shakespeare's final period was not all reconciliation and benignity but
rather that Shakespeare expressed conflict and horror in his last plays
(witness the character of Caliban).

"The Lives of the Poets" is an important piece in that it raises in a
striking way the ambiguous response to literary criticism that has
already been discussed as leading Strachey to biography. The piece
reveals Strachey's wholesale rejection of Dr. Johnson's critical judg-
ments. In Strachey's view Dr. Johnson's criticism fails to convince the
modern reader because his entire point of view is out of date. Not only
have tastes changed but, Strachey contends, modern methods of judg-

ing are different. Rather than seeing Dr. Johnson, as he surely is, as part of a great living critical tradition, Strachey characterizes him as "a standing example of a great dead tradition."[5] Strachey seeks to replace Johnson with Sainte-Beuve, the judge with the understander, yet finds himself, in spite of his own argument, drawn back toward Johnson. It was just this ambiguity about literary criticism that led Strachey to reject it in favor of biography. Oddly, Strachey found it easier to judge men than to judge their literary works. It is hard to understand why he should have thought that the two could or should be separated.

Trying to account for this change from Johnson to Sainte-Beuve, Strachey writes, "In other words, the critic discovered that his first duty was, not to criticise, but to understand the object of his criticism. That is the essential distinction between the school of Johnson and the school of Sainte-Beuve" (76). In Strachey's view this change of emphasis led to greater width and profundity. However, he points out that this method sometimes leads to an excessive concern with social and historical explanation. When this happens, he notes that the critic "sometimes forgets to mention whether the work in question has any value. It is then that one cannot help regretting the Johnsonian black cap" (76). It is ironic to see Strachey himself providing the necessary criticism of the very critical method that he prefers to the Johnson-Arnold tradition.

A similar kind of ambivalence pervades his sympathetic portrait of "Madame du Deffand" (1913). He sees her as possessing the balance and clarity of eighteenth-century style, and yet in her self-destructive passion for Horace Walpole, she is surely as romantic as the decadent romantics. This, indeed, appears to be Strachey's point of contact with the eighteenth century. Oscar Wilde and Voltaire are, perhaps, closer in their cynicism than is sometimes supposed. "Madame du Deffand" inaugurates a series of six central French pieces in the volume, four of which concern Voltaire. "Voltaire and England" (1914) shows what Voltaire learned from English liberty and civil institutions before he returned to argue for the same in France. "A Dialogue" the reader is told "is now printed for the first time, from a manuscript, apparently in the handwriting of Voltaire and belonging to his English period." It is a dialogue between Moses, Diogenes, and Mr. Locke and was imitated by Strachey in a series of comic dialogues between such unlikely people as Sennacherib and Florence Nightingale that Paul Levy has reprinted in *The Really Interesting Question* (1977).

An earlier piece, "Voltaire's Tragedies" (1905), shows how unsatisfactory Voltaire's tragedies really are. Of one of them Strachey tells the reader that Voltaire wrote to d'Alembert, "This tragedy was the work of six days," [The work enclosed was *Olympie*.] " 'You should not have rested on the seventh,' was d'Alembert's reply" (160). Indeed, it is Strachey's view that although Voltaire was daring and radical in his political thought, he was in aesthetic matters quite conservative. His tragedies are in Strachey's judgment among his least important works. "Voltaire and Frederick the Great" (1915) shows the strange relationship between these two important men of the eighteenth century. The German was drawn to the French intellectual because of an exaggerated though typically eighteenth-century respect for French culture. The central French section of *Books and Characters* closes with "The Rousseau Affair" (1907) in which the reader is told that "the unfortunate Jean Jacques was the victim, not of a plot contrived by rancorous enemies, but of his own perplexed, suspicious, and deluded mind" (204).

"The Poetry of Blake" (1906) presents the view (drawn from Strachey's Liverpool mentor Sir Walter Raleigh) that Blake "stands outside the regular line of succession" (225). But that is precisely the point, that Blake is part of a radical and original tradition that F. R. Leavis has, at least, implied runs from Blake through Dickens to D. H. Lawrence.[6] Strachey is surely right and would perhaps find Leavis in agreement with him when he writes, "But it is not as a prophet, it is as an artist, that Blake deserves the highest honours and the most enduring fame" (231). "The Last Elizabethan" (1907), already discussed, is Strachey's defense of Thomas Lovell Beddoes who, he argues, is not a minor romantic but an Elizabethan reincarnation.

This is followed by Strachey's tribute to Stendhal, "Henri Beyle" (1914), whom Strachey sees as more French than the French, and therefore not properly appreciated in France. He offers a rather implausible comparison with Shelley as someone more English than the English. The volume concludes with two portraits of English eccentrics of the kind that always interested Strachey, "Lady Hester Stanhope" (1919) and "Mr. Creevey" (1919). "Mr. Creevey" was a result of Strachey's interest in Queen Victoria for he had used Creevey's writings for his biography.

Books and Characters is important in Strachey's literary career for two reasons: first, it is probably the best collection of his literary criticism, self-selected from all the critical writings of his early career; second, it helped to solidify his position following *Eminent Victorians* and *Queen Victoria*. That a publisher would venture a selected essays, in fact, reveals how well established Strachey's reputation was by 1922.

Chapter Five

Later Career: *Elizabeth and Essex* (1928), *Portraits in Miniature* (1931), and *Characters and Commentaries* (1933)

Elizabeth and Essex (1928)

Elizabeth and Essex was mentioned by Strachey shortly after *Queen Victoria* was completed. Ironically, the triumph of *Queen Victoria* confined Strachey to his specialty. He had become a biographer. But for three years he produced very little, only beginning work on *Elizabeth and Essex* in December 1925. During this fallow period he absorbed the ideas of Freud from his younger brother James and his sister-in-law Alix who knew Freud in Vienna. James became Freud's English editor and translator as well as his brother Lytton's literary executor. Strachey uses Freudian ideas in *Elizabeth and Essex*.[1]

In August 1926 Strachey's love relationship with Roger Senhouse began. This distracted him from concentration on his book. However, the love of an older for a younger person was the subject of that book. On 11 June 1927 he wrote to his sister Dorothy, "I lead a dog's life, between Queen Elizabeth's love affairs and my own. How I survive I hardly know."[2] The book was finished a year later on 30 April 1928. As noted, Strachey had tried to write a tragedy about Elizabeth and Essex as early as 1909.

A recent popular biography (1983) of Elizabeth by Carolly Erickson treats Essex only as someone with whom Elizabeth may have dallied for a time.[3] However, Strachey's official biographer, Michael Holroyd, in his Introduction to a recent reissue of *Elizabeth and Essex*,[4] records that Strachey's popular biography has received a German stage treatment by Ferdinand Bruckner, an English stage presentation by Ashly Dykes, an American film version, and was used by William Plomer for the libretto of Benjamin Britten's opera *Gloriana*. He also compares the book to Shakespeare's *Antony and Cleopatra* in terms of parallel roles played by characters in Strachey's "tragic history" and Shakespeare's tragedy. Thus, he parallels Essex with Antony, Elizabeth with Cleopatra, Robert Cecil with Octavius, Raleigh with Lepidus, Francis Bacon (without the crisis of conscience) with Enobarbus, and Davers, Blount, Southampton, and Cuffe with Eros and Scarus. Gabriel Merle notes a further Shakespearean or Elizabethan influence in the "tragic history's" preoccupation with violence and death in the presentation of the executions of Dr. Lopez and Essex and the deaths of Philip of Spain and Elizabeth herself.[5] Also, he points out that Strachey's structure is Racinian in its classical simplicity. In terms of Strachey's personal relationship to his material Merle cites the rather brutal letter that J. M. Keynes wrote to Strachey on 3 December 1928: "You seem, on the whole, to imagine yourself Elizabeth, but I see from the picture that it is Essex whom you have got up as yourself. But I expect you have managed to get the best of both worlds."[6]

In contrast to Keynes's sense that Strachey merely expresses his personal obsession and inner division, a letter from Freud to Lytton Strachey is worth quoting here:

You are aware of what other historians so easily overlook—that it is impossible to understand the past with certainty, because we cannot divine men's motives and the essence of their minds and so cannot interpret their actions . . . You have approached one of the remarkable figures in your country's history, you have known how to trace back her character to the impressions of her childhood, you have touched upon her most hidden motives with equal boldness and discretion, and it is very possible that you have succeeded in making a correct reconstruction of what actually occurred.[7]

More than in any of his earlier works Strachey makes an effort in *Elizabeth and Essex* to integrate the work into an artistic whole through the use of poetic prose. He seems to attempt to fuse his aspirations as a poet with his work as a biographer. This attempt he dedicated appropriately to Alix and James Strachey, who were responsible, in part at least, for his interest in Freudian psychoanalysis.

The poetic prose that Strachey employs in *Elizabeth and Essex* depends upon an attempt to sustain a number of key images throughout the work rather than simply using imagery incidentally or to define central characters as he does, for example, with the eagle and dove images in the Cardinal Manning section of *Eminent Victorians*. The first important image introduced is the image of fire that is used to represent Essex as literally the last flicker of the ancient feudal flame:

Yet the spirit of the ancient feudalism was not quite exhausted. Once more, before the reign was over, it flamed up, embodied in a single individual—Robert Devereux, Earl of Essex. The flame was glorious—radiant with the colours of antique knighthood and the flashing gallantries of the past; but no substance fed it; flaring wildly, it tossed to and fro in the wind; it was suddenly put out.[8]

This is more colorful and denser prose than the balanced Voltairean writing of Strachey's early criticism. The third sentence, for example, is uncharacteristically long. Here Strachey's style develops toward the poetic in a final effort to satisfy his early aspiration to be a tragedian and poet.

However, not all the writing is in this vein; *Elizabeth and Essex* is a "tragic history" and there is historical narrative as well as tragedy to present. The reader needs to know, for example, that "Lettice Knollys's grandmother was a sister of Anne Boleyn; and thus Queen Elizabeth was Essex's first cousin twice removed. A yet more momentous relationship came into being when, two years after the death of the first Earl, Lettice became the wife of Robert Dudley, Earl of Leicester" (3) which made Essex "the stepson of Leicester, the Queen's magnificent favourite, who, from the moment of her accession, had dominated her Court" (3).

Strachey depicts his flaming feudal hero as a typically Stracheyan divided character: "The youth loved hunting and all the sports of manhood; but he loved reading too. He could write correctly in Latin and beautifully in English; he might have been a scholar, had he not been so spirited a nobleman. As he grew up this double nature seemed to be reflected in his physical complexion" (4). Essex's aptitude as soldier and scholar could be seen as fulfilling a Renaissance ideal rather than expressing a "double nature," but Strachey seems intent on establishing the psychological emphasis right away. Nevertheless, the initial emphasis favors the soldier and Essex's heroism: "In the mad charge of Zutphen he was among the bravest, and was knighted by Leicester after the action. More fortunate—or so it seemed—than Philip Sidney, Essex returned scathless to England" (4–5). There is already a parenthetical hint here of dramatic or tragic irony as there was earlier when Strachey described the flame as "suddenly put out."

Strachey notes that at the beginning of the time of the events dealt with in his book, when the relationship between Elizabeth and Essex became intense, "She was fifty-three, and he was not yet twenty" (5). Yet, he points out, "The Queen, who had known him from his childhood, liked him well" (5). As their relationship is unfolded, Essex the flame is also depicted as a star. With tragic irony already present, the reader is likely, even this early, to see Essex as a comet, meteor, or falling star. "The new star, rising with extraordinary swiftness, was suddenly seen to be shining alone in the firmament. The Queen and the Earl were never apart" (5).

A seasonal image is used by Strachey to express the change that took place in Elizabeth's reign following the defeat of the Spanish Armada in 1588. He seems to be trying to develop a poetic style to represent a poetic age: "In the place of Leicester and Walsingham, Essex and Raleigh—young, bold, coloured, brilliantly personal—sprang forward and filled the scene of public action . . . the snows of the germinating winter had melted, and the wonderful spring of Elizabethan culture burst into life" (7–8).

The difficulty of analyzing or dramatizing the inner lives of characters so distant in time and about whom there is often such scant information comes home to Strachey. Often, indeed, one senses a tiredness in his writing, probably the result of the difficulty of getting the book done and also of the fact that he was more frayed and less confident than he was when writing *Eminent Victorians* or *Queen Victoria*. "By what art are we to worm our way into those strange spirits, those even stranger bodies?" he asks (8). He worries over the strange contradictions in the Elizabethan character before concluding that "it is so hard to gauge, from the exuberance of their decoration, the subtle, secret lines of their inner nature" (10).

Having presented Essex as a character perplexed, like himself, with a double nature, Strachey also presents Elizabeth in the same way. The picture of Elizabeth I in the popular imagination is of a woman who was very strong. In contrast, Strachey presents her as someone who was, in many ways, weak and indecisive. It is not a very convincing interpretation. He depicts her first as full of "bewildering discordances of the real and the apparent" (10), and then adds, "In reality, she succeeded by virtue of all the qualities which every hero should be without—dissimulation, pliability, indecision, procrastination, parsimony" (11). He continues by presenting her temperament as a "mixture of the masculine and the feminine, of vigour and sinuosity, of pertinacity and vacillation" (12). He believes further that "Her femininity saved her" (13) and that she was the champion not of the Reformation but of the Renaissance. Her political strategy, he argues, was "To put the day of decision off—and off—and off—it seemed her only object, and her life passed in a passion of postponement" (15).

The picture that Strachey develops of Elizabeth is, indeed, one of bewildering complexity. He says, "Undoubtedly there was a touch of the sinister about her. One saw it in the movements of her extraordinary long hands" (16). Then, he goes on to note that "her crowning virtuosity was her command over the resources of words . . . the woman's inward passion vibrated magically through the loud high uncompromising utterance and the perfect rhythms of her speech" (18). However, he adds that "The tall and bony frame was subject to strange weaknesses" (19). He raises the speculation that she had "received from her father an hereditary taint" (19) but drops it in favor of his own speculation that "most of her ailments were of an hysterical origin. That iron structure was a prey to nerves" (19).

Pursuing his Freudian line of inquiry, Strachey relates Elizabeth's "problems" to her sexual nature, for he comments that "her sexual organization was seriously warped" (20). In Strachey's view, Elizabeth's emotional life had been severely strained from earliest childhood. He roots this not unreasonably in the fact that "when she was two years and eight months old, her father cut off her mother's head" (20).

Strachey links the loss of her mother to the life she led at fifteen with her stepmother Katharine Parr who had married Lord Admiral Seymour. According to Strachey, Seymour was "handsome, fascinating and reckless; he amused himself with the Princess. Bounding into her room in the early morning, he would fall upon her, while she was in her bed or just out of it, with peals of laughter, would seize her in his arms and tickle her, and slap her buttocks, and crack a ribald joke" (21). The combination of the loss of her mother and unwanted and frightening sexual attention, in Strachey's view, caused the hysteria that he mentioned earlier. The result of this was that "Marriage was distasteful to her, and marry she would not" (22).

Strachey indicates, however, that Elizabeth was not without sexual desire. He notes that she had found Seymour attractive, and further that "Her passion for Leicester dominated her existence from the moment when her sister's tyranny had brought them together in the Tower of London till the last hour of his life; and Leicester had virile beauty, and only virile beauty, to recommend him" (22–23). Strachey mentions that there were other lovers: Hatton, Henege, De Vere, and Blount.

It is at this point that he offers his Freudian-influenced analysis of Elizabeth's sexual repression:

The crude story of a physical malformation may well have had its origin in a subtler, and yet no less vital, fact. In such matters the mind is as potent as the body. A deeply seated repugnance to the crucial act of intercourse may produce, when the possibility of it approaches, a condition of hysterical convulsion, accompanied, in certain cases by intense pain. Everything points to the conclusion that such—the result of the profound psychological disturbances of her childhood—was the state of Elizabeth." (24)

Despite her expressed distaste for marriage, Strachey notes that Elizabeth would still use it as a political tool: "Her intellectual detachment and her supreme instinct for the opportunities of political chicanery led her on to dangle the promise of her marriage before the eyes of the coveting world" (24). In these two quotations one sees the essence of the division in Elizabeth's character. Strachey portrays her as both emotionally hysterical and intellectually detached. He offers the idea that, "Though, at the centre of her being, desire had turned to repulsion, it had not vanished altogether; on the contrary, the compensating forces of nature had redoubled its vigour elsewhere" (25).

In contrast to the image of Essex as a flame, Strachey presents Elizabeth's body as a castle from which she would hold her lovers at arm's length. However, he notes that even in old age she "required—and received—the expressions of romantic passion" (26). Still Strachey reinforces the image of Elizabeth as a divided person, or, at least, as a person full of contradictions: "The wisest of rulers, obsessed by a preposterous vanity, existed in a universe that was composed entirely either of absurd, rose-tinted fantasies or the coldest and hardest of facts. There were no transitions—only opposites, juxtaposed" (26).

The relationship between Elizabeth and Essex is depicted throughout as moving from quarrel to reconciliation. There is an early instance of this in section 3, where the effect is that of tragic irony: "when the Queen, from defending Raleigh, went on to attack Essex's mother, Lady Leicester, whom she particularly disliked, the young man would hear no more" (31). However, at this early stage their fascination with each other overcomes their anger and they are reconciled:

He was lavish in the protestations of his worship—his adoration—his love. That convenient monosyllable, so intense and so ambiguous, was for ever on his lips and found its way into every letter. . . . She read and she listened with a satisfaction so extraordinary, so unprecedented, that when one day she learned that he was married she was only enraged for a fortnight. (36–37)

The balanced, Voltairean style is now broken up with parentheses. Adjectival writing, repetition, antitheses are all present, and at the end there is a light, comic irony suggesting that, in his last full-length work, Strachey was trying to pull out all the stops to develop an elaborate style appropriate to a "tragic history."

More serious disagreements follow as Essex becomes entangled in political intrigues. An important figure in these entanglements is Francis Bacon whom Strachey characterizes, as he does both Elizabeth and Essex, as a complex, multifaceted personality: "It was not by the juxtaposition of a few opposites, but by the infiltration of a multitude of highly varied elements, that his mental composition was made up. He was not striped frieze; he was shot silk" (43). In fact, Bacon is characterized as a serpent. Even Bacon's writing is presented as serpentine. The reader is told that "the sage Lord Chancellor [as Bacon later became], in the midst of some great sentence, some high intellectual confection, seems to hold his breath in a rich beatitude, fascinated by the deliciousness of sheer style" (43).

Fluctuations in the relationship between Elizabeth and Essex are linked to political events such as Essex's attempt to secure the Attorney- and then the Solicitor-Generalships for Francis Bacon. In both these attempts Essex is unsuccessful. Strachey catches the oscillation of these events in the three following quotations that provide a microcosm of the rhythm of the "tragic history" at large: "The Attorney-Generalship and the fate of Francis Bacon had become entangled in the web of that mysterious amour" (56); "The lovely knight by her side had wrought the miracle—had smiled the long tale of hideous years into momentary nothingness" (57); and then "In October 1595 Mr. Fleming was appointed, and the long struggle of two and a half years was over. Essex had failed—failed doubly—failed where he could hardly have believed that failure was possible" (63). Strachey moves from politics and love through a moment of pure romance to defeat in a sequence that enacts in miniature the overall movement of the work.

In section 4 of *Elizabeth and Essex* Strachey presents, as a further instance of tragic irony, the trial and execution of the Portuguese Jew Dr. Ruy Lopez. Though Essex fails in his initial efforts to secure positions of prominence for Francis Bacon, he is successful in having Dr. Lopez charged with treason. *Elizabeth and Essex* is peppered with dashes as Strachey attempts to develop a new exclamatory and dramatic style. Thus, of Essex, the reader is told, "Enemies he must have: at home—who could doubt it?—The Cecils; abroad—it was obvious— Spain!" (68). Strachey connects Essex in his "enormous daring" and "superb self-confidence" with "The new spirit [that] was resounding, at that very moment, in the glorious rhythm of Tamburlaine; and its living embodiment was Essex" (68).

From his rationalist perspective Strachey attacks the "unenlightened" system of Elizabethan law and justice—the use of torture to extract confessions and the fact that once one was charged with treason one was almost certainly doomed. Strachey sees this as yet another instance of the duality of the age when he writes, "Thus it was that Elizabeth lived her life out, unscathed; and thus it happened that the glories of her age could never have existed without the spies of Walsingham, the damp cells of the Tower, and the notes of answers, calmly written down by cunning questioners, between screams of agony" (80).

With this situation in view, Strachey fails to provide a very satisfactory reason for Essex's hounding of poor Lopez, which is surely meant to foreshadow the death of Essex himself. Strachey characterizes Essex as an honest man, and one who would have been horrified at the idea of killing an innocent man, yet he notes "he was not very strong in the head" (80–81). This same mental weakness is later to account for Essex's own ill-fated rebellion. Strachey describes, somewhat obsessively, how Lopez was hanged, castrated, disemboweled, and quartered. Then, with a final tragic irony the section ends appropriately with Elizabeth's rather than Essex's triumph: "Elizabeth . . . took possession of King Philip's ring. She slipped it—who knows with what ironical commiseration?—on to her finger; and there it stayed till her death" (90). With this detail, Strachey reminds the reader once more of Elizabeth's propensity to play political games with the idea of marriage.

Strachey sustains the association of Essex with fire in depicting his activities with King Henry of France against Spain (91). Once again Essex's involvement in political affairs is shown to cause problems in his relationship with the Queen. The Spanish from Flanders besieged Calais and when on 14 April 1596 they took the citadel, Strachey notes: "This was too much, even for the hesitancy of Elizabeth. She could not conceal from herself that, in this instance, at any rate, she had failed; that the beautiful negation, which was the grand object of all her policy, had eluded her; that, in fact, something had actually occurred" (96). It is clear from this that Essex's love of action and Elizabeth's policy of inaction are in conflict. The siege of Calais allowed a retaliatory action, and Cadiz was stormed in June 1596. Romantic sympathy for Essex reaches its height when Strachey quotes a poem that Essex is supposed to have written on his way back from Cadiz:

> Happy were he could finish forth his fate
> In some unhaunted desert, where, obscure
> From all society, from love and hate
> Of worldly folk, there should he sleep secure;
> Then wake again, and yield God ever praise;
> Content with hip, with haws, and brambleberry;
> In contemplation passing still his days,
> And change of holy thoughts to keep him merry:
> Who, when he dies, his tomb might be the bush
> Where harmless Robin resteth with the thrush:
> —Happy were he! (105)

This wish for freedom and independence expressed in his own words makes the reader feel more fully than anywhere else in the "tragic history" that Essex can be seen as a tragic character.

Strachey then shows how Essex's success in Cadiz leads, ironically, to conflict with Elizabeth. Essex has acted vigorously, but the object of Elizabeth's policy is the perpetual postponement of action. Further, Essex's action has been expensive, and Elizabeth, Strachey has noted, is parsimonious. However, Strachey then points to the most serious cause of the Queen's displeasure: "The blaze of popularity that surrounded the Earl was not to her liking. She did not approve of anyone being popular except herself" (110). Essex has made powerful enemies in his career, notably the Cecils, who are waiting to bring him down. However, the fire imagery associated with Essex continues in Strachey's quote from Anthony Bacon: " 'Our Earl, God be thanked! . . . hath with the bright beams of his valour and virtue scattered the clouds and cleared the mists that malicious envy had stirred up against his matchless merit; he hath made the Old Fox to crouch and whine' " (113). "The Old Fox" is Lord Burghley [the elder Cecil] who is left to look for another opportunity to maneuver Essex's downfall.

Strachey's interest in the transition between different periods in history, which was noted in *Queen Victoria,* is evident again in *Elizabeth and Essex* where he depicts Essex as a symbol of the Renaissance spirit doomed to be overwhelmed by the spirit of the Reformation. He writes of Essex, "His spirit, wayward, melancholy, and splendid, belonged to the Renaissance—the English Renaissance, in which the conflicting currents of ambition, learning, religion, and lasciviousness were so subtly intervolved. He lived and moved in a superb uncertainty. He did not know what he was or where he was going" (123).

Despite Elizabeth's jealousy of his popularity, this period is the height of their relationship. Strachey, alliteratively carried away, describes their romance: "His mind, swept along by hers, danced down delightful avenues" (124). But then, as often in Strachey's writing, the tinsel of romance is stripped away to reveal an underlying cynicism: "he satisfied the peculiar cravings of a virgin of sixty-three. How was it to end?" (125). The shifting ambivalence is caught in Elizabeth's "I shall break him of his will . . . and pull down his great heart!" (128).

The turning point in this volatile relationship comes with the second expedition against Spain, which is not, unfortunately for Essex, as successful as the first. Appropriately for a "tragic history," a storm ushers in the long beginning to Essex's end. Spain is saved by the storm and "Essex himself had more than once given up his soul to God. His escape was less fortunate than he imagined; he was to be overwhelmed by a more terrible disaster; and the tempest was only an ominous prologue to the tragedy" (138–39). The reader has already been shown Elizabeth's connection with the sea, and so the sense of foreboding is intensified. There is not, however, an immediate rupture between them, for the pattern of quarrels and reconciliations continues.

On a number of occasions Strachey depicts Elizabeth as a fairy, sometimes she is Essex's "radiant fairy" but at the deathbed of Lord Burghley she is seen as "some strange old fairy daughter" (170), thus reminding the reader of Strachey's earlier observation that "there was a touch of the sinister about her" (16). Burghley's death is followed by the death of King Philip of Spain. Strachey's style of presenting King Philip's death echoes the manner he had employed in depicting Queen Victoria's death. However, the writing is less disciplined than it was in the description of Queen Victoria's death: "and so, in ecstasy and torment, in absurdity and in greatness, happy, miserable, horrible and holy, King Philip went off, to meet the Trinity" (172). The accumulation of states of being and adjectives used to describe King Philip's end gives the reader little insight into Philip's state in the face of death, and the final *h* alliterations create a sense of bathos and confusion rather than illumination. What is meant by "horrible and holy"?

As a result of turmoil in Ireland and the defeat of Elizabeth's force by the rebel Tyrone, Essex is despatched to Ireland to put down the rebellion there. Fire imagery is again important in Strachey's depiction of Elizabeth and Essex. He has Elizabeth speculate about the nature of her work, "her life's work, which consisted . . . of what? Putting out flames? Or playing with fire? She laughed; it was not for her to determine!" (183). Elizabeth has, in playing with Essex, been playing with fire; eventually, of course, she puts out his flame. At present, Ireland is in flames, and Essex is to quench the fire (see his own words to Southampton, 190)—which means, in terms of the way that Strachey has presented the imagery of the book, that he will be trying to assume Elizabeth's role which, of course, he fails to do.

Strachey notes that victory in Ireland was essential to Essex, but from the beginning things turn out badly. The fire image is now transferred to Elizabeth as though she can incorporate Essex's world whereas he is incapable of assuming ascendancy in hers. Strachey comments, "He had blown upon her smouldering suspicions, and now they were red hot" (206). When Essex finally decides to attempt to carry out Elizabeth's instructions and attack his enemy Tyrone in Ulster, he is unsuccessful and the costly enterprise ends, as Strachey puts it, with "the equivocal, accustomed triumph of Tyrone" (210). Essex then embarks from Dublin on 24 September and gallops into London on 28 September.

Strachey attempts to dramatize the ambivalence of Elizabeth's response to Essex's return: "She was surprised, she was delighted—those were her immediate reactions; but then, swiftly, a third feeling came upon her—she was afraid . . . she at once sought refuge in the dissimulation which was her second nature" (213). And so "She committed Essex to the custody of the Lord Keeper Egerton, to whose residence—York House, in the Strand—he was forthwith removed" (215).

This is, indeed, the beginning of the end for Essex. Robert Cecil, Walter Raleigh, and even Francis Bacon are now ranged against him. Elizabeth's attitude to Essex has also changed significantly as Strachey tells the reader: "For now contempt, fear, and hatred had come to drop their venom into the deadly brew of disappointed passion" (224). Essex enters into conspiracy by appealing to James of Scotland. In August 1600, however, Essex is given his liberty but Strachey notes Essex's comments on Elizabeth's conditions, " 'Her conditions are as crooked as her carcase!' The intolerable words reached Elizabeth and she never recovered from them" (233).

The outcome was that on Sunday, 8 February 1601, three hundred armed men gathered at Essex House and tried to raise the city against the court, but the city, as Strachey puts it, found that though "The Earl was their hero; . . . they were loyal subjects to the Queen" (239). The uprising failed and Essex surrendered and was sent to the Tower. The trial of Essex before his peers was held on 18 February. Francis Bacon, the man whom Essex had helped to raise, was against him. The serpent image, already noted, is used here for Bacon as Strachey writes, "One watches, fascinated, the glittering allurement; one desires in vain to turn away one's face" (245). Meanwhile, Strachey characterizes Essex as a mass of contradictions: "He loved and hated—he was a devoted servant and an angry rebel—all at once" (248). Essex is reduced to silence. Strachey implies that he is destroyed by Bacon: "Francis Bacon's task was over. The double tongue had struck, and struck again" (253).

Elizabeth is now depicted as taking over Essex's fire in order to destroy him although the castle of her own romanticism is ruined: "She was a miserable old woman of sixty-seven. She recognised the truth— the whole truth—at last. Her tremendous vanity—the citadel of her own repressed romanticism—was shattered, and rage and hatred planted their flag upon its ruins. The animosity which for so long had been fluctuating within her now flared up in triumph and rushed out upon the author of her agony and her disgrace" (257). Strachey, then, suggests a deep psychological motivation for Elizabeth's condemnation of Essex: "she condemned her lover to her mother's death" (258).

In contrast, the historian J. M. Neale in his biography of Elizabeth treats the matter in purely political terms. Essex was a rebel, therefore, he had to die.[9] Strachey, however, sees Elizabeth's execution of Essex as an attack upon manhood itself. The matter was quickly concluded. Essex's trial was completed by 19 February and his execution took place on 25 February. Finally, although he depicts Elizabeth in terms of vacillation and weakness, Strachey, like Essex, is forced to recognize her essential toughness: "Like her other victims, he realised too late that he had utterly misjudged her nature, that there had never been the slightest possibility of dominating her, that the enormous apparatus of her hesitations and collapses was merely an incredibly elaborate facade, and that all within was iron" (260). Essex's followers, Sir Christopher

Blount and Sir Charles Davers, were beheaded, and Sir Gilly Merrick and Henry Cuffe were hanged.

Strachey, drawn to the handsome Essex, makes Francis Bacon the villain of the piece. Thus, he describes Bacon's writing of his *Declaration,* in a way that resembles his own methods in *Eminent Victorians:*

By means of a clever series of small omissions from the evidence, the balance of the facts just previous to the rising was entirely changed; the Earl's hesitations—which in truth continued up to the very last moment—were obliterated, and it was made to appear that the march into the City had been steadily fixed upon for weeks. So small and subtle were the means by which Bacon's end was reached that one cannot but wonder whether, after all, he was conscious of their existence. Yet such a beautiful economy—could it have arisen unbeknownst? Who can tell? The serpent glides off with his secret. (266–67)

Strachey notes that for his services Elizabeth paid Francis Bacon twelve hundred pounds. Bacon's lack of money had been remarked throughout the book, and so the reader feels that Bacon had undertaken the task of historical revision for mercenary reasons.

The Queen is now described as old, ill, and loveless. "She sat alone, amid emptiness and ashes, bereft of the one thing in the whole world that was worth having" (276). Hers is the final tragedy, in Strachey's view, for she has lost love.

Elizabeth and Essex is as much a romantic biography[10] as a "tragic history," a romantic biography with a personal meaning for Strachey. Keynes is wide of the mark when he rather cynically suggests that Strachey attempts to get the best of both worlds by identifying with both Elizabeth *and* Essex. The personal meaning is simpler, sadder, and more poignant. *Elizabeth and Essex* is the story of a young man destroyed by an old woman. Perhaps, Strachey felt that his manhood had been denied and thwarted by a female presence that he could not get beyond. Unlike his contemporary, D. H. Lawrence, Lytton Strachey was unable to struggle free of the oedipal web. If one sees *Elizabeth and Essex* in the Freudian terms that Strachey himself used in writing the book, one might ultimately identify Elizabeth with Strachey's mother and Strachey himself with Essex.

Of all his longer biographical studies, *Elizabeth and Essex* is the one into which Strachey put most of himself, and this is the reason that he attempted to introduce a poetic prose that would allow for a fuller expression of feeling than the ironic Voltairean prose of *Eminent Victorians* and *Queen Victoria*. In *Landmarks in French Literature* Strachey had remarked that "A man's feelings are his very self, and it is around them that all that is noblest and profoundest in our literature seems naturally to centre" (192). Though Strachey's feelings may not always have been noble, it would be hard to doubt that they ran deep. He understood very well, even though he attempted to deny it in his criticism, the direct connection between personal feeling and literary expression.

Portraits in Miniature (1931)

Portraits in Miniature was the last volume that Strachey published during his lifetime. It contains just over half of the thirty or so essays that he wrote during the last decade of his life following the publication of *Eminent Victorians* in 1918. In contrast, *Characters and Commentaries* (1933) was a posthumous publication of pieces from all stages of his career, selected by his brother James, which ranged from previously unpublished early work like the "English Letter Writers" essay to his last unfinished essay on *Othello* which was begun in 1931. Many of the pieces in *Portraits in Miniature* appeared in the *Nation and Athenaeum* and *Life and Letters* between 1923 and 1928. [11]

The first of the eighteen essays in *Portraits in Miniature*, "Sir John Harington," is really a chip off the floor of *Elizabeth and Essex* in which Strachey describes a man who, like Essex, was a relative of Queen Elizabeth I. He accompanied Essex to Ireland, translated *Orlando Furioso*, and discovered the water closet—a veritable Elizabethan man of parts who the Queen herself found amusing. When Strachey describes his death it is with a touch of nostalgia for a passing age. The manner is the familiar one, that became a Stracheyan hallmark, in which he presented the death of Queen Victoria:

More and more his thoughts reverted to his old mistress. "When she smiled, it was a pure sunshine, that everyone did choose to bask in, if they could; but anon came a storm from a sudden gathering of clouds, and the thunder fell in wondrous manner on all alike." Yes! Those were great times indeed! and now . . . he was "olde and infirme"; he was forty-five; he must seek a quiet harbour and lay up his barque. [12]

The passage contains a controlling image from *Elizabeth and Essex* with Elizabeth seen by Harington in terms of cloud and storm.

"Muggleton," the second essay in *Portraits in Miniature,* is a representative piece of Stracheyan irony at the expense of religion. It is surprising, though, to see Strachey's hostility to Protestantism when one recalls his reverence for rationalism and science, for the Reformation paved the way for the triumph of both. Strachey writes, "The rule of the Catholic Church was gone, and henceforward Eternal Truth might with perfect reason be expected to speak through the mouth of any fishwife in Billingsgate. Of these prophets the most famous was George Fox; the most remarkable was Lodowick Muggleton" (11).

At the beginning of the third essay, "John Aubrey," Strachey writes, "If one were asked to choose a date for the beginning of the modern world, probably July 15, 1662, would be the best to fix upon. For on that day the Royal Society was founded, and the place of Science in civilization became a definite and recognized thing" (19). Strachey certainly saw himself as a modernist and a rationalist who believed that science was advancing the lot of mankind. Nevertheless, he shows some sympathy with Aubrey of whom he writes, "By 1670 poor Aubrey had lost everything. . . . 'I had never quiett, nor anything of happiness till divested of all,' he wrote. 'I was in as much affliction as a mortall could bee, and never quiet till all was gone, and I wholly cast myselfe on God's providence' "(21).

The lives that biographers and critics look at often help them to understand their own. It was, after all, Strachey's interest in people, which may have masked a need to understand himself, that led him to become a biographer. Of course, Aubrey was a biographer too, and Strachey describes his *Short Lives* as "one of the most readable of books." He continues, "A biography should either be as long as Boswell's or as short as Aubrey's. The method of enormous and elaborate accretion which produced the *Life of Johnson* is excellent, no doubt; but, failing that, let us have the pure essentials—a vivid image, on a page or two, without explanations, transitions, commentaries, or padding" (28). In the matter of biography Strachey's own method is much closer to Aubrey's than to Boswell's.

In contrast to the portrait of Aubrey, "The Life, Illness, and Death of Dr. North" is essentially a comic portrait of the way illness changes Dr. North. Strachey introduces him thus: "Born in 1645, the younger son of an impecunious peer, John North was one of those good little boys who, in the seventeenth century, were invariably destined to Learning, the Universities, and the Church."(30).

The following piece, "Congreve, Collier, Macaulay, and Mr. Summers," is one of Strachey's later critical efforts. He wrote less and less criticism as he turned his attention increasingly to biography. Here he argues that liberation from Victorian preconceptions has reinstated writers like the Restoration dramatists, of whom the chief, in his view, is Congreve. "As the Victorian Age grows dim on the horizon, various neglected luminaries re-emerge—among others the comic dramatists of the Restoration. The work of Sheridan begins to be taken at its true value—as a clever but emasculated *rifacimento;* the supreme master of prose comedy in English is seen to be Congreve. At least, let us hope so" (40). Strachey is happy to see Victorian prudery brushed aside: "The comedies of Congreve must be ranked among the most wonderful and glorious creations of the human mind, although it is quite conceivable that, in certain circumstances, and at a given moment, a whole bench of Bishops might be demoralized by their perusal" (49).

"Madame de Sévigné's Cousin," the sixth piece in *Portraits in Miniature,* reveals Strachey's recurrent interest in the transition from one epoch to another. His love of the eighteenth century and dislike of the Victorian period made him particularly sensitive to points of cultural and historical transition. Thus, he writes, "From about the year 1690 onwards, one begins to discern the first signs of the petrification, the *rigor mortis* of the great epoch of Louis XIV; one begins to detect, more and more clearly in the circumambient atmosphere, the scent and savour of the eighteenth century" (54). "The Sad Story of Dr. Colbatch" is different again, another instance of Strachey's interest in eccentrics and in academic rivalry.

"The Président de Brosses" resembles the first piece in *Portraits in Miniature* in one respect. Where "Sir John Harington" is a consequence of *Elizabeth and Essex,* "The Président des Brosses" is a result of Strachey's lifelong interest in Voltaire. Both are appropriately "portraits in miniature" employing, as one would expect, the method of Aubrey rather than of Boswell. The Président's claim to fame, in Strachey's view, is that he is one of the few people ever to get the better of Voltaire and at a time in Voltaire's life when he was "at last beginning to settle down to the final and by far the most important period of his immense and extraordinary career. Free, rich, happy, with his colossal reputation and his terrific energy, he was starting on the great adventure of his life—his onslaught upon Christianity" (76). Voltaire and the Président were involved in a property dispute the result of which was that "For 281 francs he [the President] had lost the immortality of the Academy. A bad bargain, no doubt; and yet, after all, the transaction had gained him another, in fact a unique distinction: he would go down to history as the man who had got the better of Voltaire" (86).

It is appropriate in a volume that deals with John Aubrey that the author whom Strachey regards as his opposite in approach to biography, James Boswell, should also be treated. The essay on Boswell is a review of Professor Chauncey Tinker's edition of Boswell's letters that Strachey regards as invaluable for understanding "the whole man". What impresses Strachey most about Boswell is his devotion to Dr. Johnson and to his *Life of Johnson.* "At the age of twenty-three he discovered Dr. Johnson" to whom he vowed " 'eternal attachment.' " Strachey adds that, "The rest of Boswell's existence was the history of that vow's accomplishment" (89). This accomplishment was achieved at tremendous cost to Boswell. Strachey notes that "He was burnt down to the wick, but his work was there. It was the work of one whose appetite for life was insatiable—so insatiable that it proved in the end self-destructive. The same force which produced the *Life of Johnson* plunged its author into ruin and desperation" (96–97).

Strachey's interest in eighteenth-century France is again evident in "The Abbé Morellet." The Abbé was a disciple of Diderot's, and Strachey once more reveals his predilection for the rational and scientific. He writes, "The great battle for liberty, tolerance, reason and humanity was in full swing; the forces of darkness were yielding more and more rapidly; and Morellet was in the forefront of the fight" (99–100).

"Mary Berry," Strachey's eleventh portrait in miniature completes an interest begun much earlier in "Madame du Deffand," the essay that Strachey had collected in *Books and Characters.* The reader learns that Horace Walpole, who had broken Madame du Deffand's heart in her old age, is himself smitten in old age by Mary Berry. Strachey's interest in unrequited love is personal as he suffered throughout his life from that feeling. Now the feeling that plagued Madame du Deffand and to a degree Queen Elizabeth I attacks Walpole. Strachey notes the intensification of the feeling in old age: "Love grows cruel as he grows old; the arrow festers in the flesh; and a pleasant pang becomes a torture" (111). For Strachey, Walpole and Mary Berry also symbolize the eighteenth century, and Horace Walpole's *Reminiscences* (1788) cause Strachey to reflect upon an eighteenth century that seems more like a polished and superficial social illusion than reality.

Though she breaks Walpole's heart, quite unwittingly, in Mary

Berry the eighteenth century lives on into the nineteenth, and provides
Strachey with another of his cultural transition figures: "The *salon* in
Curzon Street lasted on into the Victorian age, and Thackeray would
talk for hours with the friend of Horace Walpole . . . When, in 1852,
both [Berry] sisters died, aged eighty-nine and eighty-eight, the eighteenth century finally vanished from the earth" (118).

The final miniature portrait that precedes his section on "Six English
Historians," is of Madame de Lieven who was born in 1785. Strachey
informs the reader, "From the first moment of her existence she was in
the highest sphere" (122). His fascination with social surfaces which
pervades his writing is fully displayed here. He notes that Madame
"could be very entertaining in four languages" and that "Whenever she
appeared, life was enhanced and intensified" (123). The piece, like a
good deal of the rest of Strachey's social description, reads like a society
gossip column, as Madame Lieven's four-year affair with Metternich,
Lord Grey's admiration of her, and her friendship with Guizot are
cataloged.

It is with some relief that one turns to "Six English Historians." It
must have been a source of satisfaction to Strachey at the end of his life,
and after his early failure to win a history fellowship at Trinity College,
Cambridge, or to get his work on Warren Hastings published, to be
commissioned to write essays of this kind. The six historians who
Strachey treats are Hume, Gibbon, Macaulay, Carlyle, Froude, and
Creighton. Needless to say, because of Strachey's predilections the two
eighteenth-century historians receive much fairer treatment than the
four from the nineteenth century.

Hume is praised as the great rationalist. Writing of the *Treatise of
Human Nature* (1738), Strachey argues that:

The book opened a new era in philosophy. The last vestiges of theological
prepossessions—which were still faintly visible in Descartes and Locke—were
discarded; and reason, in all her strength and all her purity, came into her
own. It is the sense that Hume gives one of being committed absolutely to
reason—of following wherever reason leads, with a complete, and even reckless, confidence—that the great charm of his writing consists. (143)

However, despite the initial failure of the *Treatise* and the immediate
success of Hume's *History of England,* Strachey judges Hume a much
better philosopher than historian. Indeed, he argues that "The virtues
of a metaphysician are the vices of a historian. A generalised, colour-

less, unimaginative view of things is admirable when one is considering the law of causality, but one needs something else if one has to describe Queen Elizabeth" (147). Strachey appears to be speaking from recent experience. His attempt to color his style in *Elizabeth and Essex* would seem to issue from an attempt to suit style to subject.

It is Gibbon who fulfills Strachey's ideal. Indeed, Gibbon occupies a place in Strachey's pantheon alongside Racine, Voltaire, and Horace Walpole. For Strachey, Gibbon symbolizes all that is best in the eighteenth century, "One sees in such a life an epitome of the blessings of the eighteenth century—the wonderful $\mu\eta\delta\grave{\epsilon}\nu$ $\check{\alpha}\gamma\alpha\nu$ (nothing in excess) of that balmy time—the rich fruit ripening slowly on the sun-warmed wall, and coming inevitably to its delicious perfection. It is difficult to imagine, at any other period in history, such a combination of varied qualities, so beautifully balanced—the profound scholar who was also a brilliant man of the world—the votary of a cosmopolitan culture, who never for a moment ceased to be a supremely English 'character' " (156). Strachey's idealization of the eighteenth century is a cultural-social fantasy cherished, it seems, because of its "perfect form."

The attempt to come to terms with Gibbon's achievement leads Strachey to question the nature of history as a subject. He concludes that it is an art rather than a science. This allows him to praise Gibbon as a great artist. He writes, "That the question has ever been not only asked but seriously debated, whether History was an art, is certainly one of the curiosities of human ineptitude. . . . it is obvious that History is not the accumulation of facts, but the relation of them" (160). Strachey argues, therefore, that a great historian is necessarily a great artist. In Gibbon's case, he believes, "his History is chiefly remarkable as one of the supreme monuments of Classic Art in European literature" (161).

Commenting on the difficulty of writing history, Strachey notes that "Gibbon's central problem was one of exclusion: how much, and what, was he to leave out?" (162). It is a difficulty that he himself had faced in writing *Eminent Victorians*. Strachey goes on to note the importance of style in this regard: "The style once fixed, everything else followed" (163). While admitting that Gibbon's style is exclusive and "bars out a great multitude of human energies" (163), Strachey feels that the classic beauty achieved is worth the price. He defends Gibbon against the nineteenth century's criticism of him by remarking that the nineteenth century "did not relish the irony beneath the pomp" in Gibbon's work. In writing of Gibbon's irony and also of Voltaire's, he identifies the sources of his own irony, for Voltaire and Gibbon were his mentors in this kind of writing.

Having praised Gibbon, Strachey finds it easy to attack Macaulay for "A coarse texture of mind—a metallic style—an itch for the obvious and the emphatic—a middle-class, Victorian complacency" (169). However, Strachey admits that by "sheer power of writing" Macaulay overcomes these limitations. In discussing Macaulay, Strachey pursues his interest in style since he sees in style the clue to understanding the nature of an author. So of Macaulay he writes, "The style is the mirror of the mind, and Macaulay's style is that of a debater" (175). Still on the subject of the relationship of the mind and the style, Strachey notes, "in Macaulay's case, one cannot resist the conclusion that the absence from his make-up of intense physical emotion brought a barrenness upon his style. His sentences have no warmth and no curves; the embracing fluidity of love is lacking" (177). In contrast to his earlier effort as a critic to separate life and art, Strachey seems to realize here that the style is, indeed, the man, that Macaulay's style reveals his inner nature just as Strachey's sometimes exaggerated, sometimes hysterical, often ironic style reveals his.

Concluding his discussion of Macaulay, Strachey reiterates his belief in the importance in history not of the accumulation of facts, "but the relation of them" (160). He remarks, "History is primarily a narrative, and in power of narration no one has ever surpassed Macaulay. . . . His whole History is conditioned by a supreme sense of the narrative form" (178–179).

It is probably fair to say that Carlyle is a representative Victorian and that this is the reason why Strachey dislikes and misrepresents him. On a familiar note, Strachey comments that "the Victorian spirit, had brought about a relapse from the cosmopolitan suavity of eighteenth-century culture; the centrifugal forces, . . . had triumphed, and men's minds had shot off into the grooves of eccentricity and provincialism" (181–182). Strachey identifies Carlyle with this change.

While Strachey insists on Carlyle's "insularity," he does not see it as a source of his strength: "Carlyle was not an English gentleman, he was a Scotch peasant; and his insularity may be measured accordingly—by a simple sum in proportion. . . . on the whole he is, with Dickens, probably the most complete example of a home growth which the British Islands have to offer the world" (182). Strachey's assessment of Carlyle smacks of snobbery. Yet he admits that his generation's dismissal of Carlyle is perverse: "The northern lights, after all, seem to give out no heat, and the great guns were only loaded with powder. So, at any rate, it appears to a perverse generation" (183).

Strachey's "perverse" argument is that, "What was really valuable in Carlyle was ruined by his colossal powers and his unending energy" (184). He rejects Carlyle's importance as a prophet or Victorian sage and insists that Carlyle is only important as "a historian and a memoir writer, and it is safe to prophesy that whatever is permanent in Carlyle's work will be found in that section of his writings" (184).

The injustice of Strachey's judgment of Carlyle grows directly out of his antipathy to the Victorian age and to his continuous preference for manners over morality. To read Strachey's miniature portrait of Carlyle is to read another chapter in *Eminent Victorians*:

The stern child of Ecclefechan held artists in low repute, and no doubt would have been disgusted to learn that it was in that guise that he would win the esteem of posterity. He had higher views: surely he would be remembered as a prophet. And no doubt he had many of the qualifications for that profession— a loud voice, a bold face, and a bad temper.

. . . .

Perhaps if Carlyle's manners had been more polished his morals would have been less distressing. Morality, curiously enough, seems to belong to that class of things which are of the highest value, which perform a necessary function, which are, in fact, an essential part of the human mechanism, but which should only be referred to with great circumspection. (185–87)

Strachey's criticism of Carlyle's manners is merely a piece of gratuitous snobbery at the expense of a "Scotch peasant." His obvious antipathy to Carlyle makes it difficult for the reader to accept his judgment that Carlyle had "a true gift for history which was undone by his moralisations" (188).

In "Froude" Strachey attacks another of "the salient figures in mid-Victorian England" (195). In his effort to understand Froude he asks, "What was the inner cause of this *brio* and this sadness, this passionate earnestness and this sardonic wit?" (195–196). Strachey suggests that fuller knowledge of modern psychology can help us to understand these Victorians better than they understood themselves. Science, Strachey believes, might have freed Froude; that it would have been better for Froude to have submitted himself to science than to Carlyle. Indeed, Froude seems to be used merely as another stick with which to beat Carlyle. Strachey's discussion of Froude is hobbled by the same snobbery that weakened his discussion of Carlyle. "The bias, no doubt, gives a spice to the work, but it is a cheap spice—bought, one feels, at the Co-operative Stores. The Whiggery of Macaulay may be tiresome, but it has the flavour of an artistocracy about it, of a high intellectual tradition; while Froude's Protestantism is—there is really only one word for it—provincial" (204–5). This is Strachey at his worst—the Bloomsbury snob with a limited understanding of anything outside his own circle.

The final portrait in miniature and the last of the "Six English Historians" series is "Creighton." It is another Stracheyan hatchet job on a Victorian historian whose work Strachey describes thus, "In his work a perfectly grey light prevails everywhere. . . " (209). Strachey damns Creighton's historical writing with faint praise: "The biscuit is certainly exceedingly dry; but at any rate there are no weevils in it" (210). In short, stabbing sentences Strachey attempts to belittle Creighton the Victorian. "He believed in the Real Presence. He was opposed to Home Rule. He read with grave attention the novels of Mrs. Humphry Ward" (212). But unless one shares Strachey's antipathy to all things Victorian, the attack lacks force. Ironically, the final estimate of Creighton almost has the effect of a backhanded compliment: "Firmly fixed in the English tradition of commonsense, compromise, and comprehension, he held on his way amid the shrieking of extremists with imperturbable moderation" (216). Indeed, the "Six English Historians," especially the final four Victorians, brings Strachey's writing, published in his lifetime, to an appropriate conclusion. The wheel turns full circle. Strachey ends where he began and where he is best known—as a detractor of the Victorian age that produced him.

Characters and Commentaries (1933)

Characters and Commentaries (1933) offers another means of providing a concluding review and summary of Strachey's achievement. It was edited by his brother James who down to his death in the mid-sixties was an extremely faithful literary executor. Besides *Characters and Commentaries,* James prepared a selection of his brother's *Spectator* reviews called *Spectatorial Essays* (1964), edited the correspondence of his brother and Virginia Woolf, saw to it that a uniform edition of his brother's principal works was published, and generously encouraged scholars of his brother's work such as Professor Sanders from the United States who published the first full-length study in 1957, Michael Hol-

royd whose official biography appeared in the late 1960s, and Gabriel
Merle from France whose two-volume study appeared in 1980. James
Strachey, the English editor and translator of Freud, did a great deal to
keep his brother's memory green.

Many of the pieces in *Characters and Commentaries,* which appeared
the year after Strachey's death, have been discussed already. Suffice it to
say that the book is divided into four sections that reflect accurately the
development of Strachey's career as a writer and that it contains a
selection of those uncollected pieces that James Strachey felt, at his
brother's death, were worth collecting. Section 1 consists of Strachey's
"English Letter Writers" (1905), the previously unpublished long essay
or short book in six chapters that Strachey had submitted unsuccess-
fully for the Le Bas prize at Cambridge. This is followed by nine early
essays and reviews published between 1903 and 1908 in the *Independent
Review,* the *Speaker,* the *Albany,* and the *New Quarterly.*

Taken together these pieces reveal that Strachey was interested in
writing biographical portraits in miniature as early as 1904. Favorite
characters of Strachey's such as Horace Walpole, Mademoiselle de
Lespinasse, and Lady Mary Wortley Montagu with their sad love stories
and eighteenth-century elegance are already present here. The third
section includes fourteen pieces published between 1913 and 1918 that
show Strachey both as a literary reviewer and as a critic of World War I.
The volume concludes with a selection of nine later essays written and
published between 1919 and 1931 that range from "Shakespeare at
Cambridge" (1919), which is commentary by the *Spectator*'s former
drama critic on an amateur postwar production of Shakespeare that
favors simple, natural presentation over the artificialities of the West
End, through Strachey's Leslie Stephen lecture at Cambridge (1925) on
Pope to Strachey's last unfinished essay on *Othello* of 1931. What
Strachey left unfinished at his death was a series of essays on Shakespeare and an extended piece of work on his hero, Voltaire.

Chapter Six
Conclusion

Following Strachey's death in January 1932, his reputation increased slowly through the 1930s and '40s fostered by the interest of sympathetic scholars who were often aided by his brother James's generous cooperation. Up to the present an increasing stream of previously unpublished and reprinted material has appeared in which there has been a good deal of scholarly interest. In conclusion, it will be useful to consider these developments and try to estimate Strachey's literary place and significance.

During the 1930s, after the appearance of *Characters and Commentaries* (1933), little new material of Strachey's was published. James Strachey wisely chose to bide his time rather than flood the market with reprints or previously unpublished material. So, apart from a poem that appeared in the *Saturday Review of Literature* and three that were printed in the *New Statesman and Nation* in June 1937, the most significant item to appear during the 1930s was the eight-volume *Greville Memoirs* (1814–1860), on which Strachey had worked during the last years of his life. It was published by Macmillan's of London in 1938 with notes and commentaries done by Strachey in collaboration with Roger Fulford. Fulford remarks that "The notes are almost all Mr. Strachey's."

After World War II a handsome *Collected Works* in six volumes was published by Chatto and Windus of London (1948). Many readers will be familiar with this uniform set that contains: *Landmarks in French Literature; Eminent Victorians; Queen Victoria; Elizabeth and Essex;* and two volumes selected by James Strachey of *Biographical Essays* and *Literary Essays*. As James Strachey points out in a Biographical Note, the contents of *Books and Characters: French and English* (1922), *Portraits in Miniature* (1931), and *Characters and Commentaries* (1933) are reduced in *Biographical Essays* and *Literary Essays* from three volumes to two and are redistributed to reflect the two sides of Strachey's career. Half a dozen items are dropped and a piece on Greville added.

Six years later, in 1956, Leonard Woolf and James Strachey brought out a volume of correspondence between Lytton Strachey and

Virginia Woolf that was published jointly by the Hogarth Press and Chatto and Windus. This was followed eight years later by James Strachey's selection of his brother's *Spectatorial Essays* published by Chatto and Windus in a volume uniform with the *Collected Works*. Then in 1969 Anthony Blond of London published an illustrated edition of Strachey's *Ermyntrude and Esmeralda* which was introduced by Michael Holroyd whose definitive biography of Strachey had just appeared. Two years later this was followed by *Lytton Strachey By Himself: A Self-Portrait,* a selection of previously unpublished material including extracts from Strachey's journal chosen by his biographer Michael Holroyd and published by Heinemann.

Judicious selection of previously unpublished material continued with Paul Levy's *The Really Interesting Question and Other Papers* (London: Weidenfeld & Nicholson, 1977) for which Levy had selected items from Strachey's papers delivered to the Apostles and other Cambridge societies. This was followed in 1980 by *The Shorter Strachey,* selected and introduced by Michael Holroyd and Paul Levy who, following the deaths of James and Alix Strachey, became literary executors of Strachey's papers for the Strachey Trust. The volume provides a useful introduction to Strachey's work. However, much Strachey material remains unpublished. In particular, his voluminous correspondence has not yet been edited. Michael Holroyd plans a selection in two volumes for the late 1990s. Also, although twice produced, Strachey's tragic melodrama, "A Son of Heaven," is still unpublished. It seems unlikely, then, that any kind of complete works will appear before the next century.

Although sure foundations have been laid in recent decades, much editorial and critical work on Strachey remains to be done. One can foresee a complete letters and eventually a complete works with supporting or related critical studies that consider such questions as Strachey's role in the new biography, his place in the Bloomsbury group or in the tradition of anti-Victorianism.

Work on Strachey in the twenty-five years following his death necessarily tended, despite James Strachey's generous support, to be preliminary, tentative, or both. The first extended study to appear after the obituary tributes of 1932 was Clifford Bower-Shore's *Lytton Strachey: An Essay* (1933). Bower-Shore praises Strachey for his clear French style which he sees as adding balance and charm to the English tradition. He admires Strachey's contribution to the art of biography, and particularly praises *Eminent Victorians* and *Queen Victoria*. He does not find *Elizabeth and Essex* successful.

In the same year Bonamy Dobrée published an essay simply titled "Lytton Strachey" in W. R. Inge's volume *The Post Victorians* (1933). Like Bower-Shore, Dobrée finds *Elizabeth and Essex* the weakest of Strachey's books because of an obsession with sex that spoils Strachey's detachment. Also, like Bower-Shore, Dobrée sees Strachey's chief importance as an iconoclast who freed the generation after World War I from a Victorian stranglehold. Dobrée believed, besides, that Strachey's main contribution to literature was not as a stylist but as someone who had helped improve the art of biography.

In 1935 Guy Boas's English Association pamphlet no. 93 concerned Lytton Strachey. In it he argued that *Queen Victoria* was the most impressive of Strachey's achievements, better balanced than *Eminent Victorians,* and much more successful than *Elizabeth and Essex* in which, Boas felt, Strachey was out of his depth. Just before World War II the first book-length study, K. R. S. Iyengar's *Lytton Strachey: A Critical Study* (1939), appeared. Iyengar points out that there was a well-developed anti-Victorian tradition before Strachey—a tradition rooted within the Victorian age itself. Like Bower-Shore and Dobrée, Iyengar emphasizes Strachey's contribution to biography. On the question of style, Iyengar quotes Charles Smyth's critical questioning in the *Criterion* (July 1929, 655) of Strachey's style: "Is it a vein of effeminate timidity that makes it almost impossible for him to use a noun without qualifying it with an adjective.?"[1] While this certainly points to a weakness in Strachey's style—an excessive use of adjectives—the phrase "effeminate timidity" is both irrelevant and offensive.

Max Beerbohm's Rede Lecture (1943) finds the dedicatee of *Portraits in Miniature* also stressing the importance of Strachey the biographer. He calls attention to Strachey's admiration for the eighteenth century. A decade later J. K. Johnstone's *The Bloomsbury Group: A Study of E. M. Forster, Lytton Strachey, Virginia Woolf and their Circle* (1954) appeared. Johnstone's intention was "to see the novels of Virginia Woolf and of E. M. Forster, and the biographies of Lytton Strachey, in their relation to the Bloomsbury milieu." This initiated an approach continued by Sanders, Holroyd, and Merle that helped the reader more and more to see Strachey's life and work in the context of his environment and time. Johnstone stresses the importance of works like G. E. Moore's *Principia Ethica* (1903) for understanding what he calls "Bloomsbury Philosophy" with its emphasis on personal affection and aesthetic enjoyment.

He stresses the influence of Roger Fry. Johnstone suggests that Strachey is best seen as an essayist since he favored this form of expression throughout his literary career. Like previous commentators, Johnstone finds *Elizabeth and Essex* the least successful of Strachey's full-length works.

R. A. Scott-James's British Council pamphlet no. 65 appeared in 1955. Scott-James stresses Strachey's stylistic debt to both English and French eighteenth-century writers like Gibbon and Voltaire. He singles out *Landmarks in French Literature* for special praise, though he values *Queen Victoria* most highly of Strachey's works. He, too, is unimpressed by *Elizabeth and Essex*. In 1957 Charles Richard Sanders, in his *Lytton Strachey: His Mind and Art,* set a new standard for work on Strachey. Appearing a quarter of a century after Strachey's death, Sanders's book provides a full biographical sketch of Strachey. Sanders had earlier published a family history, *The Strachey Family, 1588–1932* (Duke University Press, 1953). Also, he treats in detail various aspects of Strachey's work as critic and biographer. In the early chapters of the book he concentrates on Strachey as critic; then, he turns to Strachey the biographer. Strachey's roles as critic, biographer, and stylist are all fully discussed. The book concludes with "A Chronological Check List of Lytton Strachey's Writings." In 1957 it was by far the most comprehensive work on Strachey that had appeared. It was prepared with James Strachey's support and cooperation.

Four years after Sanders's work, Martin Kallich's *The Psychological Milieu of Lytton Strachey* appeared. As its title suggests, it concerns Strachey's debt to Freud and links Strachey's work to a tradition that runs back through Sainte-Beuve to Suetonius and Plutarch. Kallich wishes to understand Strachey's handling of psychology as a means of estimating his contribution to biography. He sees psychoanalysis as an important development in modern thought and concludes that Strachey's "major contributions to biographical analysis are part of this massive psychological trend."[2] He quotes a letter that he received from James Strachey testifying to Lytton's increasing interest in psychoanalysis that culminated in *Elizabeth and Essex,* the work dedicated to James and his wife.

In 1963 an important thesis on Strachey was accepted by the University of Minnesota graduate school. This is G. K. Simson's "Lytton Strachey's Use of His Sources in *Eminent Victorians.*" Simson's is a very helpful and detailed work that enables the reader to see both how Strachey deployed and how he distorted his sources in *Eminent Victorians.*

The 1960s was, of course, a crucial decade for studies of Lytton
Strachey because of the appearance in 1967 and 1968 of Michael Holroyd's two-volume biography, which is probably the most important
work on Strachey to have appeared to date. It provides us with an
almost day-to-day account of Strachey's life and emerges from Holroyd's careful sifting of everything Strachey has written, including his
voluminous unpublished correspondence. Holroyd's account of the
years he spent on the Strachey biography is contained in the single
volume Penguin edition (1971), "Preface To The Revised Edition." A
decade later Gabriel Merle's two-volume *Lytton Strachey (1880–1932):
Biographe et Critique d'un Critique et Biographe* (1980) was published in
Paris. Like Holroyd's biography, Merle's biographical and critical
study of a critic who became a biographer depends upon full acquain-
tance with and copious quotation from all the unpublished material. It
is a rich resource for any serious student of Strachey's life and writing.

Merle's study was followed a year later by Michael Edmonds's *Lytton
Strachey: A Bibliography* that is invaluable for finding out about editions
of Strachey's work and the location of unpublished material. Edmonds
argues that "Strachey's main contribution to English literature lies in
his rejuvenation of the field of biography. Lamenting the formless,
multi-volume 'lives and letters' which eulogized many nineteenth-
century worthies, Strachey proposed that biographers use judgment
and discrimination to create characteristic portraits of their subjects. . . . He shifted the focus of biography from the subject's accom-
plishments to his or her motives and inner dynamics, and tried to reveal
the psychological bases underlying his subject's actions."[3]

In attempting to estimate Lytton Strachey's literary place and significance, it is helpful to recall Gabriel Merle's placing of Strachey in the
literary pantheon somewhere between Horace Walpole and Charles
Lamb. Merle's placing suggests several things; first, that Strachey is a
minor writer and someone who may come to be best known as an
essayist or letter writer; second, that Strachey, like Walpole and Lamb,
typifies in his writing and personality a particular period in English
literary history. As Walpole is characteristic of the late eighteenth
century and Lamb a characteristic romantic figure, so Strachey helps to
characterize what was happening in English letters at the beginning of
this century. Though Walpole, Lamb, and Strachey are all minor, they
are representative.

It is possible to characterize Strachey as a minor modern ironist,
Edwardian belletristic critic, or Bloomsbury aesthete, but it would be

fairer to see him as an iconoclast who helped to break down the Victorianism that lingered into the Edwardian period and beyond. Better still, one can see him as an essayist who helped to rehabilitate Racine's reputation in England, or best as a writer who helped to give English biography a new lease on life. Lytton Strachey is unlikely to be forgotten, even if he is remembered as an irritant who, struggling to determine who he was, helped others to realize who they were. He will always be remembered for some of the things he said. The iconoclasm of *Eminent Victorians* will always be recalled when Strachey's name is mentioned.

Notes and References

Chapter One

1. For fuller accounts of Strachey's life and the history of his family see Michael Holroyd, *Lytton Strachey: A Biography* (Harmondsworth: Penguin, 1971); Gabriel Merle, *Lytton Strachey (1880–1932): biographe et critique d'un critique et biographe,* 2 vols. (Paris: Librairie Honore Champion, 1980); C. R. Sanders, *The Strachey Family, 1588–1932: Their Writings and Literary Associations* (Durham, N.C.: Duke University Press, 1953); and Barbara Strachey, *The Strachey Line* (London: Gollancz, 1985).

2. See "Lancaster Gate" in *Lytton Strachey By Himself; A Self-Portrait,* ed. Michael Holroyd (London: Heinemann, 1971).

3. Strachey was dressed by his mother in petticoats in his early years, which may well have contributed to his problems with sexual identity. See Holroyd, *A Biography,* 63. His French governess was Marie Souvestre. Ibid, 56 ff.

4. See *Lytton Strachey By Himself: A Self-Portrait,* 38–78; hereafter cited in the text as *SP* followed by page number.

5. See Paul Levy, *Moore: G. E. Moore and the Cambridge Apostles* (London: Weidenfeld & Nicholson, 1979), for a full account of this society.

6. See Robert Skidelsky. *John Maynard Keynes: Hopes Betrayed 1883–1920* (London: Macmillan, 1983), for a full account of the friendship between J. M. Keynes and Lytton Strachey.

7. See C. R. Sanders, *Lytton Strachey: His Mind and Art* (New Haven: Yale University Press, 1957), 23–24.

8. See Letters to Duncan Grant. British Library Additional MS 57932 (1902–18).

9. Ibid.

10. See James Strachey, "Preface" to Lytton Strachey, *Spectatorial Essays* (London: Chatto & Windus, 1964).

11. Correspondence with James Strachey, British Library MS 60706–60712.

12. See Paul Levy, "Introduction" to Lytton Strachey, *The Really Interesting Question and Other Papers* (London: Weidenfeld & Nicholson, 1972), xiii.

13. Merle, *Lytton Strachey,* 120, amusingly includes the quotation besides, that in Bloomsbury "all the couples were triangles and lived in squares." The "bi-sexual *ménage à trois*" was briefly for Carrington, Ralph, and Strachey a "Triangular Trinity of Happiness." See Merle, 220.

14. Ibid., 210.

15. See Holroyd, *A Biography*, 994–95.

16. See Merle, *Lytton Strachey*, 647, quoting a letter that Keynes wrote to Strachey on 3 December 1928 in which he observes, "You seem, on the whole, to imagine yourself as Elizabeth, but I see from the picture that it is Essex whom you have got up as yourself. But I expect you have managed to get the best of both worlds."

17. Martin Kallich, *The Psychological Milieu of Lytton Strachey* (New Haven: College & University Press, 1961), 14, quotes James Truslow Adams's observation that "What we get is Strachey's reaction to his sitter. When, for example, for four pages, he recounts the thoughts that pass through Elizabeth's mind, we are getting fiction as pure and undefiled as anything Thackeray tells us about Becky Sharp."

18. See Merle, *Lytton Strachey*, 760.

19. See Holroyd, *A Biography*, 1058.

20. See Merle, *Lytton Strachey*, 764.

21. See Michael Holroyd and Paul Levy, "Introduction" to *The Shorter Strachey* (London: Oxford University Press, 1980), xii.

22. See F. R. Leavis, "Keynes, Lawrence and Cambridge" and "Keynes and Currency Values" in S. P. Rosenbaum, ed., *The Bloomsbury Group: A Collection of Memoirs, Commentary and Criticism* (London: Croom Helm, 1975), 387–401.

Chapter Two

1. *Characters and Commentaries* (London: Chatto & Windus, 1933), 3; hereafter cited in the text as *CC* followed by page references.

2. *Books and Characters: French and English* (New York: Harcourt Brace & Co., 1922), 53–54; hereafter cited in the text as *BC* followed by page references.

3. See Letters to Duncan Grant. British Library Additional MS 57932 (1902–18).

4. Correspondence with James Strachey, British Library MS 60706–60712.

5. See Holroyd, *A Biography*, 860–62.

6. Introduction to Mrs. Inchbald, *A Simple Story* (London: Henry Frowde, 1908), in *CC*, 134–47.

7. *Spectatorial Essays*, 114.

8. See Merle, *Lytton Strachey*, 367–87. His account of *Landmarks in French Literature* is extremely perceptive and has been invaluable to me throughout.

9. *Landmarks in French Literature*, Home University Library of Modern Knowledge Series (London: Williams & Norgate (1912), 102; subsequent page references will be given in parentheses in the text.

Chapter Three

1. See Merle, *Lytton Strachey,* 407.

2. Strachey wrote poetry all his life from 1885 until a few weeks before his death. He wrote about 5,000 poems in all, but only ten were published during his lifetime. Merle categorizes them as imitations, pastiches or parodies, and poems about death and sexual poems. Almost all are rhymed with the exception of *Essex: A Tragedy* in which Strachey attempts blank verse.

3. See Merle, *Lytton Strachey,* 440.

4. See Merle's discussion of biography, ibid., 446–77.

5. See Ian Ker, review of Robert Gray, *Cardinal Manning: A Biography* (London: Weidenfeld & Nicholson, 1985), in *Times Literary Supplement,* 7 February 1986.

6. See Edmund Gosse, *Anglo-Saxon Review* 8 (1901): 195–208. "We in England bury the dead under the monstrous catafalque of two volumes (crown octavo), and go forth refreshed, as those who have performed a rite which is not in itself beautiful, perhaps, but inevitable and eminently decent. . . . The two great solemn volumes . . . follow the coffin as punctually as any of the other mutes in perfunctory attendance."

7. *Eminent Victorians* (Harmondsworth : Penguin, 1984), 9; subsequent page references will be given in parentheses in the text.

8. See *Characters and Commentaries,* 203.

9. See G. K. Simson, "Lytton Strachey's Use of his Sources in *Eminent Victorians,*" dissertation, University of Minnesota, 1963, which is extensively cited by Gabriel Merle in his discussion of *Eminent Victorians.*

10. *Cardinal Manning,* 6–7.

11. See Merle, *Lytton Strachey,* 497–98.

12. See Merle, *Lytton Strachey,* 500. Merle suggests that Sir Edward Cook's essay "The Art of Biography," *National Review* 63 (April 1914): 266 ff. strongly influenced Strachey's biographical method in *Eminent Victorians.* Cook emphasized the importance of artistry, brevity, and lack of pedantry.

13. Merle, *Lytton Strachey,* 522.

14. Letter cited by Merle, ibid.

15. Ibid., 522–23.

16. See Aldous Huxley, "The Author of *Eminent Victorians*" in *On The Margin* (London: Chatto & Windus, 1923), 141–47.

17. Simson, "Strachey's Use of his Sources," 1963 dissertation.

18. See Merle, *Lytton Strachey,* 542.

19. Ibid., 543.

20. Ibid., 549.

21. Ibid., 553.

22. See Merle, *Lytton Strachey,* 557, who summarizes the arguments both for and against.

23. Ibid., 562.

Chapter Four

1. *Queen Victoria* (London: Chatto & Windus, 1921), 18; subsequent page references will be given in parentheses in the text.
2. See Merle, *Lytton Strachey*, p. 42 n. 77, p. 771, where he quotes Lady Strachey's letter to her son of 10 January 1919: "I don't much fancy you taking up Queen Victoria to deal with. She no doubt lays herself open to drastic treatment which is one reason I think it better left alone."
3. Merle, *Lytton Strachey*, 571.
4. See Robert Rhodes James, *Albert, Prince Consort* (London: Hamish Hamilton, 1983), 82.
5. *Books and Characters: French and English* (New York: Harcourt, Brace & Co., 1922), 75; subsequent page references will be given in parentheses in the text.
6. This is surely the implication of F. R. Leavis's later work on Blake, Dickens, and D. H. Lawrence. See in particular the essay on *Little Dorrit* in *Dickens the Novelist* (London: Chatto & Windus, 1970) and *Thought, Words and Creativity: Art and Thought in Lawrence* (London: Chatto & Windus, 1976).

Chapter Five

1. See Merle, *Lytton Strachey*, 615.
2. Ibid., 616.
3. See Carolly Erickson, *The First Elizabeth* (London: Macmillan, 1983), 386–97.
4. Michael Holroyd, Introduction to Lytton Strachey, *Elizabeth and Essex* (London: Oxford University Press, 1981), xiv.
5. See Merle, *Lytton Strachey*, 629.
6. Ibid., 647.
7. Merle, (ibid., 655) cites Holroyd's biography, vol. 2, 615–16.
8. *Elizabeth and Essex: A Tragic History* (London: Chatto & Windus, 1928), 2; subsequent page references will be given in parentheses in the text.
9. See Merle, *Lytton Strachey*, 648.
10. As a romantic biography, it is of interest that *Elizabeth and Essex* first appeared in monthly installments in the *Ladies' Home Journal* between September and December 1928, before its publication in book form. See Merle, *Lytton Strachey*, 850.
11. Merle, *Lytton Strachey,* 668.
12. *Portraits In Miniature* (London: Chatto & Windus, 1931), 8; subsequent page references will be given in parentheses in the text.

Chapter Six

1. K. R. S. Iyengar, *Lytton Strachey: A Critical Study* (London: Chatto and Windus, 1939), 113.

2. Martin Kallich, *The Psychological Milieu of Lytton Strachey* (New Haven: College and University Press, 1961), 44.

3. Michael Edmonds, *Lytton Strachey: A Bibliography* (New York and London: Garland, 1981), xvi.

Selected Bibliography

Within each section of the Bibliography items appear chronologically according to the date of publication.

PRIMARY SOURCES

Michael Edmonds, *Lytton Strachey: A Bibliography*. New York and London: Garland, 1981. Includes the many locations of Strachey manuscript material and his unpublished correspondence.

1. Books

"Ely: An Ode." In *Proclusionae Academicae*. Cambridge: Cambridge University Press, 1902.

Euphrosyne: A Collection of Verse. Cambridge: Elijah Johnson, 1905.

Landmarks in French Literature. Home University Library. London: Williams & Norgate; New York: Henry Holt, 1912.

Eminent Victorians. London: Chatto & Windus; Garden City, N.Y.: Garden City Publishing Co., 1918.

Queen Victoria. London: Chatto & Windus; New York: Harcourt, Brace & Co., 1922.

Pope (The Leslie Stephen Lecture). Cambridge: Cambridge University Press, 1925.

Elizabeth and Essex: A Tragic History. London: Chatto & Windus; New York: Harcourt, Brace & Co., 1928.

Portraits In Miniature and Other Essays. London: Chatto & Windus; New York: Harcourt, Brace & Co., 1931.

Characters and Commentaries. With a preface by James Strachey. London: Chatto & Windus; New York: Harcourt, Brace & Co., 1933.

The Greville Memoirs. Edited with Roger Fulford (Joint editors: Ralph and Frances Partridge). 8 vols. London: Macmillan, 1937–38.

The Collected Works. (Landmarks in French Literature; Eminent Victorians; Queen Victoria; Elizabeth and Essex; Biographical Essays; Literary Essays). 6 vols. London: Chatto & Windus, 1948.

Virginia Woolf and Lytton Strachey: Letters. Edited by Leonard Woolf and James Strachey. London: Hogarth Press and Chatto & Windus, 1956.

Spectatorial Essays. With a preface by James Strachey. London: Chatto & Windus, 1964.

Ermyntrude and Esmeralda: An Entertainment. Introduced by Michael Holroyd. London: Anthony Blond, 1969.

Lytton Strachey By Himself: A Self-Portrait. Edited and introduced by Michael Holroyd. London: Heinemann, 1971.

The Really Interesting Question and Other Papers. Edited and introduced by Paul Levy. London: Weidenfeld & Nicholson, 1972.

The Shorter Strachey. Selected and introduced by Michael Holroyd and Paul Levy. London: Oxford University Press, 1980.

2. Articles and Reviews

C. R. Sanders. *Lytton Strachey: His Mind and Art* (1957) contains the excellent "A Chronological Check List of Lytton Strachey's Writings" and Gabriel Merle. *Lytton Strachey (1880–1932): Biographe et Critique d'un Critique et Biographe* (1980) contains an excellent chronology of "Oeuvres de Lytton Strachey" in which all Strachey's articles and reviews are listed together with their dates and places of publication and subsequent collection.

SECONDARY SOURCES

1. Books

Huxley, Aldous. "The Author of *Eminent Victorians.*" In *On The Margin,* 141–37. London: Chatto & Windus, 1923. An early discussion by an important contemporary.

Thurston, Marjorie H. "The Development of Lytton Strachey's Biographical Method." Dissertation, University of Chicago, 1929. The first full-length study.

Bower-Shore, Clifford. *Lytton Strachey: An Essay.* London: Fenland Press, 1933. The first full-length study to be published. It discusses Strachey's French-influenced style and his contribution to biography.

Dobreé, Bonamy. "Lytton Strachey." In *The Post Victorians,* edited by W. R. Inge, 577–89. London: Nicholson & Watson, 1933, Stresses Strachey's importance as an iconoclast and contributor to the art of biography.

Swinnerton, Frank. *The Georgian Scene.* New York: Farrar & Rinehart, 1934. Describes the author's excitement on first reading the manuscript of *Eminent Victorians* for Chatto & Windus.

Boas, Guy. *Lytton Strachey.* The English Association Pamphlet, no. 93, November 1935. Stresses the importance of *Queen Victoria.* Sees it as Strachey's finest achievement.

Köntges, G. *Die Sprache In Der Biographie Lytton Stracheys.* Marburg-Lahn: Herman Bauer, 1938. The first study not written in English.

Iyengar, K. R. *Lytton Strachey: A Critical Study.* London: Chatto & Windus, 1939. Stresses Strachey's relation to anti-Victorianism and his contribution to the art of biography.

Clemens, C. *Lytton Strachey.* Webster Groves, Mo.: International Mark Twain Society, 1942. The first published American study.

Beerbohm, Max. *Lytton Strachey* (The Rede Lecture). Cambridge: Cambridge University Press, 1943. Stresses Strachey's importance as a biographer and admirer of the eighteenth century.

Keynes, John Maynard. *Two Memoirs.* London: Hart-Davis, 1949. Impressions by Strachey's Cambridge friend.

Cecil, David (Lord). "Lytton Strachey." In *Dictionary of National Biography, 1931–40,* 835. London: Oxford University Press, 1949. Standard biographical entry.

Sanders, C. R. *The Strachey Family, 1588–1932: Their Writings and Literary Associations.* Durham, N. C.: Duke University Press, 1953. A detailed family biography down to Strachey's death.

Johnstone, J. K. *The Bloomsbury Group: A Study of E. M. Forster, Lytton Strachey, Virginia Woolf and their Circle.* London: Secker & Warburg, 1954. Studies Strachey and his Bloomsbury colleagues against the background of the "Bloomsbury Philosophy" of G. E. Moore and Roger Fry.

Scott-James, R. A. *Lytton Strachey.* British Council, Writers and their works, no. 65. London: Longmans Green & Co., 1955. Stresses Strachey's debt to the English and French eighteenth century. Values *Queen Victoria* most highly of Strachey's works.

Sanders, C. R. *Lytton Strachey: His Mind and Art.* New Haven: Yale University Press, 1957. The first fully detailed and extended study that set the study of Strachey on a new footing. Contains the excellent, "A Chronological Check List of Lytton Strachey's Writings," 355–66.

Yu, M. S. *Two Masters of Irony: Wilde and Lytton Strachey.* Foreword by Edmund Blunden. Hong Kong: Hong Kong University Press, 1957. The first Oriental study.

Kallich, Martin. *The Psychological Milieu of Lytton Strachey.* New Haven: College & University Press, 1961. Explores Strachey's debt to Freud and the relationship between psychoanalysis and "the new biography."

Simson, G. K. "Lytton Strachey's Use of his Sources in *Eminent Victorians.*" Dissertation, University of Minnesota, 1963. An excellent account of how Strachey draws upon and distorts his sources in his best-known work.

Holroyd, Michael. *Lytton Strachey: A Critical Biography, Volume I: The Unknown Years 1880–1910.* London: Heinemann, 1967. The first volume of Holroyd's definitive biography of Strachey.

————. *Lytton Strachey: A Critical Biography, Volume II: The Years of Achievement 1910–1932.* London: Heinemann, 1968. The second volume of the definitive biography of Strachey. The two volumes were revised and published by Penguin as *Lytton Strachey: A Biography,* and *Lytton Strachey and The Bloomsbury Group: His Work, Their Influence* (London: Penguin, 1971).

Carrington: Letters and Extracts from her Diaries. Chosen and introduced by David Garnett. London: Jonathan Cape, 1970. Writings by Dora Carrington, the woman with whom Lytton Strachey spent the last fifteen years of his life.

The Bloomsbury Group: A Collection of Memoirs, Commentary and Criticism. Edited by S. P. Rosenbaum. London: Croom Helm, 1975. An important collection of writings by and about members of the Bloomsbury group.

Darroch, S. J. *Ottoline: The Life of Lady Ottoline Morrell.* London: Chatto & Windus, 1976. Biography of Lady Ottoline Morrell with whom Strachey was closely associated during the war years and after.

French Boyd, Elizabeth, *Bloomsbury Heritage: Their Mothers and Their Aunts.* London: Hamish Hamilton, 1976. Contains a chapter on Lytton's mother, Lady Strachey, 48–75.

Edel, Leon. *Bloomsbury: A House of Lions.* London: Hogarth Press, 1979. A wide-ranging study of nine members of the Bloomsbury group. Contains "A Bloomsbury Chronology 1885–1920," 279–80.

Levy, Paul. *Moore: G. E. Moore and the Cambridge Apostles.* London: Weidenfeld & Nicholson, 1979. A study of the philosopher whose *Principia Ethica* (1903) influenced the Bloomsbury group. It includes an account of the Apostles of whom Strachey was a member.

Garnett, David. "Lytton Strachey and Carrington." In *Great Friends: Portraits of seventeen writers,* 150–59. London: Macmillan, 1979. An account of Lytton and Carrington by a contemporary who knew them both.

Merle, Gabriel. *Lytton Strachey (1880–1932): Biographe et Critique d'un Critique et Biographe.* 2 vols. Paris: Librairie Honore Champion, 1980. An extremely full and detailed study that draws upon unpublished material and offers important insights into many areas of Strachey's work. Contains excellent chronologies and bibliographies. With Holroyd's biography, the most important study of Strachey published so far.

Edmonds, Michael. *Lytton Strachey: A Bibliography.* New York and London: Garland, 1981. An extremely helpful bibliography of Strachey's writings that includes locations of manuscript material.

Skidelsky, Robert. *John Maynard Keynes: Hopes Betrayed 1883–1920.* Vol. 1. London: Macmillan, 1983. Detailed biography of Strachey's Cambridge friend. Contains new material on Strachey's early life.

Strachey, Barbara. *The Strachey Line.* London: Gollancz, 1985. A new family biography.

Bloomsbury / Freud: Letters of James and Alix Strachey 1924–1925. Edited by
Perry Meisel and Walter Kendrick. London: Chatto & Windus, 1985.
Recently published letters by Strachey's brother and sister-in-law.
Annan, Noel. *Leslie Stephen: The Godless Victorian.* London: University of
Chicago Press, 1986. Stephen's influence on the Bloomsbury group.

2. Articles, Reviews
Gabriel Merle. *Lytton Strachey (1880–1932): Biographe et Critique d'un Critique
et Biographe* (1980) possesses an excellent "Bibliographie Critique" (854–
80) that lists articles on and reviews of Strachey's writing.

    Études Anglaises 4 (October-December 1980) is almost a Lytton
Strachey centenary issue containing useful articles by Michael Holroyd,
Gabriel Merle, Paul Levy, and George Simson.

Index